The Ephesian Tradition

The Ephesian Tradition

An Oral Source of the Fourth Gospel

By H. E. DANA

President and Professor of New Testament
Interpretation in the Kansas City
Baptist Theological
Seminary

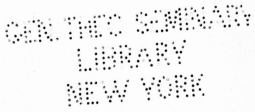

The Kansas City Seminary Press

1 9 4 0

Copyright 1940 by

H. E. DANA

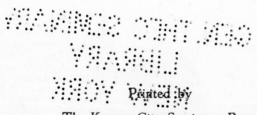

Printed by

The Kansas City Seminary Press

Kansas City, Kansas

U. S. A.

TO CHARLES BRAY WILLIAMS

From whom the author received
his first insight into critical
interpretation of the New
Testament

PREFACE

The investigation of the oral sources of the Gospels, which has been brought into prominence and perspective by the *Formgeschichte* school of German scholars, is necessarily and inescapably of a highly subjective character. It is a process of seeking for the most plausible conjectures. This treatise represents an effort to apply this new method of Gospel criticism to the sources of the Fourth Gospel. Hence the following pages are expected to be regarded as in the nature of hypothetical suggestion, offered for the scrutiny and criticism of New Testament scholarship. The author would be far from finality for any of the conclusions proposed. Dogmatism has never a place anywhere in the realm of critical inquiry, and certainly not in Gospel criticism at its present stage of progress. Objective phenomena have been thoroughly and repeatedly canvassed until there has emerged practical agreement as to what they are—such as the appearance of Mark in the records of Matthew and Luke; the material, chiefly discourse, common to Matthew and Luke, but not found in Mark; the differences of the Fourth Gospel from the Synoptics, and its distinctive style of the teachings of Jesus, which is the style of the narrative portions of the Gospel and of I John; etc. As soon as we begin pursuit of the question as to what inferences can be derived from these phenomena, we are launching into a realm of hypothesis, which is essentially subjective. Here dogmatic conclusions are necessarily out of place. Hence finality is not claimed for any of the findings offered in this discussion. The author will be highly gratified if he

7

has but indicated some directions for further study of the Fourth Gospel.

The hypothesis here presented should be submitted to a test which this writer is not sufficiently prepared to apply. This necesary test is the question, how far Aramaic reflections appear in those parts of the Gospel which have been ascribed to Palestinian sources. Such a test would not be final for or against the theory we have defended, but obviously it would have important weight.

The first intimation of this hypothesis presented itself to the mind of the author as far back as 1927. After pursuing the study of it at intervals for twelve years, and when the first draft of a formal manuscript was nearing completion, there came to his attention the remarkable brief work by P. Gardner-Smith, *St. John and the Synoptic Gospels* (Cambridge University Press, 1938), and to his delighted surprise he discovered that the British scholar had been proceeding toward a conclusion closely related to his own. Professor Gardner-Smith's work supports a chief premise of the thesis presented in this book; namely, that the wide differences of John's Gospel from the Synoptics are such as to preclude a tenable supposition that John made use of the Synoptic Gospels, all or any of them, as a source. It will be found that nearly every page of Gardner-Smith's work has been documented in this one. The author wishes to record his profound appreciation of the splendid contribution of the British scholar.

A paper on "The Stratification of Tradition in the Fourth Gospel", prepared a few years ago for the Midwestern Branch of the Society of Biblical Literature and Exegesis, and later published in the *Journal of Religion,* has been employed in the preparation of this book. The author wishes to register his thanks to the editorial staff of the *Journal of Religion* for permission to use this material. He also is indebted to Dean Ernest Cadman Colwell and Professor Donald Wayne Riddle of the University of Chicago for helpful suggestions and encouragement. Mr. George H. Hink, Superintendent of the Kansas City Seminary Press, has kindly taken a personal interest in the printing of the book.

H. E. Dana

Seminary Heights,

Kansas City, Kansas.

THE EPHESIAN TRADITION: AN ORAL
SOURCE OF THE FOURTH GOSPEL

— I —

Critical investigation which has now been in progress for more than a century has demonstrated that the
materials which compose our Synoptic Gospels are
derived from many sources. The exact limits and contents of these sources is a matter of wide difference of
opinion, so that we may not well hope for any general
agreement as to their precise number, but scholarship is
practically agreed that there were two *types* of sources
from which our Gospel materials came—oral and written.
It is also a matter of universal agreement that the original
form was oral.[1] This view may be regarded without
question as a securely established result of criticism. In
fact no other view can successfully be maintained in the
light of the phenomena of the Gospels and the known
customs of the times. Doubtless for at least twenty-five
years following the Resurrection this oral tradition remained the only form of the Gospel history. Some time
about the middle of the first century this oral deposit of
apostolic reminiscence began to be reduced to documentary form.

We can conclude with fair certainty *when* gospel
writing began by considering *why* it began. It is a fair
conjecture that this process of reducing evangelic tradition to writing appeared within the first decade after

1 More than a half century ago Renan observed: "La tradition vivante
était le grand réservoir où tous puisaient". Les Evangeles, p. 96.

11

Christianity began to spread in the Gentile world. The Jew was so habituated and adept in the use of oral tradition that he had little need of transmission by the written page. It may be regarded as a practical certainty that not a line of gospel material was written in Palestine during the first century. Palestinian Jews did not write: they depended on oral transmission. But not so with the Greek. Writing was the fixed custom of the first century Græco-Roman world.[2] As soon as the first Christian missionaries began to teach their Gentile converts a demand arose for Christian literature, for a Gentile would want it written out where he could see it. The rapid adaption of the Christian mission to its environment is demonstrated at so many other points that it is not reasonable to doubt it here. This demand for the written page by the Greek converts to Christianity and the first Greek teachers in the churches was the original and most potent cause of gospel writing, but many other motives entered in, appearing successively with the advancing development of first century Christian life.[3]

When Greek converts began to ask for the oral tradition in written form, their demands were readily supplied. Various teachers would write out the oral tradition, as each was himself taught and found need in his own teaching, and thus many "Gospel Lessons" arose. These Gospel Lessons were composed of brief compendia of sayings of Jesus, or groups of traditional narratives. They mark the first stage of Gospel writing. We may safely regard Luke's "many gospels" as embracing such Gospel

2 Flinders Petrie, **Growth of the Gospels, pp. 4-8.**
3 An excellent discussion of these additional motives may be found in Grant, **Growth of the Gospels,** pp. 45-52.

Lessons. It is not mere fancy to suppose that we can detect such Gospel Lessons in Mk. 1:21-45; 2:1-3:6; 13:1-37; 14:12-15:47, etc. The first could have been a Gospel Lesson on the healing ministry of Jesus, the second on his conflict with the Pharisees, the third on his pro-phetic teachings, and the fourth a passion story. These were certainly distinct matters of community interest. In some such form we must suppose that the evangelic docu-ments first began to appear, and multiply until the language of Lu. 1:1 became applicable in strict literalness. We have cited four possible examples from Mark by way of illustration: the number could be greatly expanded.[4] To think of Mark's Gospel as an innovation in gospel writing is destined to become increasingly difficult as Gospel criticism advances.

It might have been expected that the Gospel Lessons would have superseded the oral tradition, but such was not the case. The two continued to serve side by side in the instruction of Gentile converts. It was the Gospel Lessons which were destined to be displaced. This was done by the Primitive Gospels. We are using the term "Primitive Gospel" to designate a second step in Gospel writing, when a small number of Gospel Lessons were compiled into a longer and more or less connected story of Jesus. Here Gospel production was moving in the direction of the Greek model of history writing, which was a most important development, since it is exceedingly doubtful whether our Four Gospels would ever have come into existence had not apostolic Christianity come under the influence of such Greek literary methods.[5]

---

4   Vincent Taylor, Formation of the Gospel Tradition, pp. 175-185.
5   Cadbury, Making of Luke-Acts, pp. 127-134.

Among the earliest of these Primitive Gospels was doubtless a copy of the Mathean *Logia* mentioned by Papias. Another was probably a collection of narratives which was employed later as a historical setting for teaching material by the author of the first Gospel. Then there was perhaps another employed by Luke in his Gospel, chapters ix to xviii. With fair assurance we may class the Gospel of Mark among these Primitive Gospels: that is, we would place it at the second stage in Gospel writing. This then creates the hypothesis that we have from this second stage of gospel writing, which we call Primitive Gospels, four survivals: the Matthean *Logia,* the Matthean Narratives (M), a "Proto-Luke", and Mark. Whatever documents of Passion Narratives may have been in use would most probably belong to the earliest stage of literary production, the Gospel Lessons.

Representing a third stage in gospel writing there appear our Gospels of Matthew and Luke. Using some of the Primitive Gospels, of which there must have been several, interspersed with oral tradition, and perhaps scattered contributions from the Gospel Lessons, our first and third evengelists produced the two larger and more carefully organized accounts of the ministry of Jesus which we have in our New Testament canon.

This description of the beginnings of gospel writing is of course largely conjectural, but we believe if offers a workable hypothesis in seeking to reconstruct that vital process of literary history. We expect to establish at least the strong probability that the Fourth Gospel was a continuation of this process.

For the past fifty years New Testament scholarship has all but exclusively been interested in this process of documentary formation. Indeed, some critics have seemed to lose sight of the fact that there ever was an oral tradition. Researches of our own century have called us back to the recognition that the evangelic material in its original form was "evidently an oral tradition, not fluid but fixed, and evidently learned by all Christians when they entered the church".[6] This oral tradition not only preceded the written Gospels, but paralleled them as a highly respected source of evangelic history until far into the second century. Papias quite evidently had a partiality for the oral sources, and tradition was still the chief source of Christian instruction when the book of Hebrews was written, as is attested by the emphasis upon "the things heard" in 2:1. Many other evidences testify to the long survival of the oral tradition, as we shall subsequently observe.

In the past three decades the attention of New Testament scholarship has been focused anew upon this oral tradition. This dissertation is offered as a contribution to this realm of investigation, especially as it applies to the Fourth Gospel, a hitherto neglected field.

6 Goodspeed, **Introduction to the New Testament**, p. 126.

II

An important caution in approaching this study is not to revert to the opposite extreme from that which has characterized Gospel research of the latter part of the nineteenth century, and ignore the significance of the documentary developments. It is hardly wise to dismiss all the results of documentary research by declaring summarily that "all such attempted solutions are quite uncertain".[1] Our knowledge of these developments must indeed remain hypothetical, but not any more so than the findings of *Formgeschichte*.

There are certain conclusions of literary criticism of the Gospels which may be accepted as reasonably secure. We may be sure that Mark was the first of our canonical Gospels written, and was based at least primarily upon oral tradition. We have observed above the possibility of its having incorporated some documentary sources, but we can never have more than plausible conjecture for the foundation of such a theory. Mark's Gospel was reproduced almost *in toto* by Matthew and Luke, who also without reasonable doubt employed other documentary sources. A document of sayings was common to the two, which was perhaps an early edition of "Matthew" — the Matthean *Logia*.

Light on the beginnings of gospel production is reflected in the description by Papias of the background of Mark and Matthew. He certainly means to describe Mark as a written Gospel, but it is quite doubtful that

1 Bultmann in Grant, **Form Criticism**, p. 14.

we could accurately apply that term to the document he ascribes to Matthew. The term he employs (συνεγράψατο) rather suggests a compilation of sayings, and some question has been raised as to whether he meant to describe a written document at all.[2] We may well believe that these *Logia* had composed a discourse tradition, promoted among the Jewish Christian churches of Syria under the leadership of the Apostle Matthew, and hence known as "Matthew's Logia". Papias tells us that these sayings were variously translated. One such translation was made by an unknown hand, and was circulated as "Matthew's Gospel", or a title which developed into that designation. This was later combined with material from Mark and other sources in the production of a larger Gospel bearing the same or a similar title. We may also plausibly suppose it to have been one of Luke's "many gospels". Peter carried a similar though briefer tradition to Rome, interspersed doubtless with his own reminiscences. This tradition constituted a principal basis for Mark's Gospel. Then Mark and the earlier edition of "Matthew" constituted a common basis for our present canonical Matthew and Luke.

This account is of course highly conjectural, but it is related to an assumption which may be regarded as one of the most secure findings of modern Gospel criticism: that Matthew and Luke are based upon two common written sources, Mark and a discourse document. That there was any other common documentary source of Matthew and Luke we cannot conclude with

2 Goodspeed, op. cit., pp. 129, 174.

any high degree of certainty.[3] Besides Mark and the discourse document, which we will designate λ for convenience, Luke seems to have had at least one other source, probably two. Scholarship of today quite generally agrees that a document lies behind Lu. 9:51-19:27. This source we will call L. Luke's Passion Narrative shows an independence which has led many scholars to assign it to a distinct written source. This hypothetical Passion document we may designate π. Matthew also had an independent documentary source which we shall follow Streeter in calling M,[4] though we believe it originated in Syria or Galilee rather than Jerusalem.

As a simplified working hypothesis we adopt the following analysis of documentary sources.

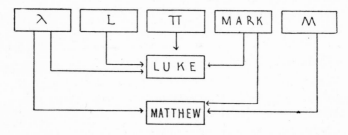

---

3 But **per contra** see Burton, **Some Principles of Literary Criticism and the Synoptic Problem**; supporting, see Cadbury, **The Making of Luke-Acts**, pp. 62ff.

4 Streeter, **The Four Gospels**, pp. 232ff.

III

Our next inquiry is, may we distinguish the separate oral sources from which these documents arose? Was there but one oral tradition, employed in fixed and unvarying form throughout all Palestine and Hellenistic Christianity? We regard this as an impossible hypothesis. Palestinian and Hellenistic tradition must first be distinguished. The investigations of *Formgeschichte* have not kept clearly enough in view the fact that our Greek Gospels are at a third distinct step from the original Palestinian tradition. They are based upon documentary sources, with some oral elements incorporated; these documentary sources are based upon a Hellenistic Christian tradition; and the Hellenistic Christian tradition is a transmutation (not a translation) of an original Palestinian tradition.[1] The Palestinian tradition was carried by the first Christian missionaries into the Hellenistic world and re-wrought into a Greek tradition. The Greek of the Synoptic Gospels exhibits Semitic traces, enough to attest Palestinian origin for the material, but the records are far too Hellenistic in general character to be mere translations from Aramaic.

Evidences of the modifying effects of Hellenism upon the original Aramaic tradition may be seen in the narration of the miracles of Jesus in the Greek "Miracle-story" form.[2] However, it is to be observed that the so-called Greek form of miracle story is but the very natural form for such narratives to assume, independent of any dis-

1 Cadbury, **op. cit.**, p. 62.
2 Bultmann in Grant, **op. cit.**, p. 36.

tinctive literature to which it might belong.[3] Nevertheless, the presence of the Greek mode of narration in this case must be more than mere co-incidence. Wide comparison by competent and honest investigators reveals unquestionable parallels of form in this case, and in view of the fact that Gentile Christian tradition was molded in a Greek environment it is most reasonable to assume that these parallels reveal an essential relationship. We must recognize here a modifying influence of Hellenistic forms of expression.

There also appears the Greek form of introduction, the more impressive because it is found right along-side the Semitic form. In introducing the parable of the Good Samaritan Luke (10:25ff.) presents the question of the scribe in good Semitic form, ἀνέστη ἐκπειράζων αὐτὸν λέγων. The introduction of the rejoinder of Jesus looks quite typically Greek, ὁ δὲ εἶπεν πρὸς αὐτόν, but the answer of the scribe reverts to Semitic idiom again, ὁ δὲ ἀποκριθεὶς εἶπεν. In a parallel to the last mentioned clause Matthew has ὁ δὲ ἔφη αὐτῷ (22:37) and Mark, ἀπεκρίθη ὁ Ἰησοῦς ὅτι (12:29), both in good Greek form. Examples could be many times multiplied. The mingling of Greek and Semitic idiom in the Synoptic Gospels is abundantly evident, and points to an original Aramaic source transferred into the Greek speaking world.

Nor should we too hastily conclude that there was but one Hellenistic tradition. Any opinion on this question must wisely be left tentative for the present, in the absence of conclusive evidence, but two competitive lines of tradition are surely intimated in the background of Ac.

3 Richardson, The Gospels in the Making, p. 109.

18:25, 26. Here Luke does not deny that Apollos was a true follower of Christ, as he does in the case of the twelve disciples in the following record (19:1-7). He acknowledges that Apollos was "instructed in the way of the Lord". The Greek here is significant (κατηχημένος τὴν ὁδὸν τοῦ κυρίου). It signifies instruction in oral tradiion.[4] The tradition in which Apollos had been instructed had only one defect. It was "informed (ἐπιστάμενος) only as to the baptism of John". It contemplated only water baptism, and was not "informed" as to the baptism of the Holy Spirit. Luke, influenced by the Pauline viewpoint, regarded the latter as the more important. Hence he considered the tradition in which Priscilla and Aquila instructed Apollos as "more accurate". Here appear two Hellenistic traditions, harmonious in fundamental substance, but with a different history behind each and at least one essential variance. This contains a forceful suggestion relative to the original Palestinian tradition and its transference into the Hellenistic world. It at least presents strong confirmation of the inherent probability that there was more than one Hellenistic Christian tradition.

Then was there but one original body of tradition for all Palestine? Such a supposition disregards well known facts of first century Jewish life. Galilean and Judean Judaism were distinct in many respects—in character, in interests, in customs.[5] This fact is too familiar to require detailed discussion. Likewise, there are subtle but significant evidences that Galilean and Judean Christianity ex-

4 But **per contra**, see Cadbury in Faokes Jackson and Lake, **Beginnings of Christianity**, vol. ii, p. 508f.

5 Edersheim, **Life and Times of Jesus the Messiah**, pp. 355, 555, etc.

perienced many differences. That Galilee as well as Judea
had distinct Christian communities is now recognized
by practically all writers on the beginnings of Christianity.[6] The traditional view that post-Resurrection
Christianity consisted wholly in the church at Jerusalem
and its scattered members must be abandoned when we
give due regard to all the evidence.

The impression has come to prevail that the Jerusalem church included all the disciples of Jesus after the
Resurrection because the book of Acts accords so little
attention to the disciples elsewhere. But it is to be
observed that Acts itself records the presence of Christianity throughout western Palestine. In 9:31 we have the
brief but explicit statement that after the conversion of
Paul "the church throughout all Judea and Galilee and
Samaria had peace". The Western text of Acts reads,
"the churches", and there is strong reason for looking
favorably upon this reading. The use of the singular,
"the church", as embracing the Christian communities of
an entire district, reflects a late Christian conception which
appears anachronous in the book of Acts. Such an application was in accord with a universal use of the term
by the time the earliest of our existing New Testament
manuscripts was produced, so it is not difficult to see how
the plural could have been changed to the singular, but
highly improbable that the singular would have been
changed to the plural. The Alexandrian and Caesarean
texts both arose under strong ecclesiastical influence, so
we regard the Western text at this point as the more
primitive. However, the textual point is not important,

6 Enslin, **Christian Beginnings**, p. 169.

since either reading witnesses to the presence of Christian disciples in Galilee a few years after the Resurrection. Bacon questions the historical reliability of this record,[7] but with Luke's manifestly slight interest in Galilee he could hardly have had any motive for describing the presence of Christians there except that it was a known fact. And his testimony is supported by other strong inferences.

We cannot reasonably suppose that when Jesus left Galilee and started on his last journey to Jerusalem he was followed by all his true Galilean disciples. Indeed, we must infer from the Synoptic Gospels that the very reverse was true. Hundreds of earnest followers remained in Galilee. The news of their Master's death by crucifixion was undoubtedly a shock to their faith in his Messiahship and a momentary deterrent to their devotion. But the Resurrection experiences were granted to Galilean as well as Judean disciples (Mk. 14:28; Mt. 28:16; Jn. 21:1). Hence they too must have taken up the apparently defeated cause, to revive and promote it in the name of the one whom they regarded as a risen Lord.

Observe that Luke accounts for only a hundred and twenty as witnesses of the Ascension and participants in the experiences of Pentecost. These become in his account the nucleus of Jerusalem Christianity. No one would assume that these represented the total number of the faithful disciples left by Jesus. The simple fact is, we have Paul's unqestionable testimony to the contrary. He mentions an appearance of the risen Christ to "over five hundred brethren" (I Cor. 15:6). Certainly some of these

7 **The Journal of Religion**, xi, p. 507.

were Galileans, and competent scholarly opinion favors the view that the appearance was in Galilee.

Another strong possibility pointing toward the fact of Galilean disciples is the undoubted presence of Galileans among those who espoused the Christian cause as a result of the first Pentecost after the Resurrection. After the first period of Messianic excitement and expectancy of the immediate return of Jesus had subsided, the Galilean disciples would naturally drift back to their original homes, and thereby swell the number of the disciples left there by Jesus when he departed for the last Passover.

Further confirmation may be inferred from the known presence of churches closely adjacent to the Galilean territory. Luke records certain visits of Paul to communities of Christian disciples in Tyre, Sidon and Ptolemais (Ac. 21:4,7; 27:3). The remains of an ancient church were found at Sephoris in 1931 by the University of Michigan Institute of Archaeological Research. Of course such a church edifice could not have been erected earlier than a hundred years after the Apostolic Age, but it attests to a survival of Christianity in Galilee, and therefore its existence there at an earlier period.[8]

None of these inferences standing alone would be conclusive, but when combined into single perspective they have a cumulative force which should be accepted as confirming the simple testimony of Luke in Ac. 9:31. We find ourselves quite convinced that there were Christian disciples in Galilee when the Gospel tradition was in

---

8 This same evidence the author has presented in his **Jewish Christianity,** pp. 27-29. Compare also Foakes Jackson, "The Acts of the Apostles" in **The Moffatt New Testament Commentary,** p. 85.

process of formation, and these Galilean disciples certainly had a tradition.

That there were Judean churches outside Jerusalem is so well attested that it were gratuitous to propose corroborative inferences. The conclusion is supported by the testimony of both Luke and Paul (Ac. 8:1; 9:31; Gal. 1:22; I Thes. 2:14). Distinct Christian communities existed at Lydda and Joppa, for we have record of Peter visiting them (Ac. 9:32,36). Hence we may safely proceed on the assumption that there were Judean churches and Galilean churches, with characteristic differences between the Christian communities in the two localities.

When we examine the phenomena of the Gospel text we find convincing evidence that these distinct areas of Palestinian Christianity formulated distinct evangelic traditions. In general substance these traditions were of course parallel, but in form, detailed content and emphasis there were pronounced differences, characteristic of their origin. The Galilean churches were more interested in the activity of Jesus in Galilee, while his infrequent contacts with Judea were magnified by the Judean disciples. This variance of local interest is obviously reflected in the Gospel text. The clashes of Jesus with standard Judaism appear more drastic in Judean tradition, where Judaism was more dogmatic and more sensitive to deviations than in Galilee. Thus the severe denunciations of the Pharisees were preserved in Judean tradition. They appear in L and λ, and L was composed primarily of Judean tradition, while λ was chiefly Galilean with Judean contributions. The Passion Narrative was more vivid and elaborate in Judea, the scene of the events. The

Galilean tradition contained the Galilean appearances of the risen Lord, while Judea preserved an account of the appearances about Jerusalem. There were variations in the formulation of distinct sections of tradition representing the same event or teaching, as we see in the records of the Lord's Prayer, the Call of the First Disciples and the Sermon on the Mount. In the Lord's Prayer Matthew follows λ, while Luke prefers his Judean source L, as often he does is such parallels; in the Call of the First Disciples Matthew follows Mark in the use of a Galilean source. while Luke again prefers L; in the Sermon on the Mount Matthew is probably incorporating λ practically unaltered, while Luke has employed another source for the entire discourse—Luke's variant source here being most likely Judean, since it is less elaborate and vivid than that of Matthew, which was derived from Galilee, the original scene of the teachings contained in the Sermon on the Mount. In subsequent discussions we shall observe quite an array of phenomena in the Gospel text which points in this direction.

We now summon Paul as a witness to a distinct Judean tradition. That Paul propagated a body of oral tradition in his ministry is abundantly attested. The "traditions" for loyalty to which Paul commends the Corinthians (I Cor. 11:2) must properly be regarded as embracing the oral tradition of the life and teaching of Jesus, for in two other places in his Corinthian correspondence Paul unquestionably refers to such a tradition. His description of the Lord's Super (I Cor. 11:23-26) is designated as a traditional heritage. The word rendered "delivered" in I Cor. 11:23 contains the same root from which the Greek word for tradition is derived. We may properly paraphrase the passage thus: "From authentic sources connected directly with the Lord I received the tradition which I passed on to you". The word rendered "received" is παρέλαβον, which signifies to receive by transmission from others, through oral tradition or instruction of teachers.[9] When we compare Luke's account with that of Paul on one hand and that of Mark on the other (Mk. 14:22-25; Lu. 22:14-23), we find Luke has a conflation of the two which leaves his record confused— presenting the cup twice. Upon examination of the textual evidence we find that there is variance and confusion at this point, some manuscripts omitting Lu. 22:19b, 20, which throws Luke's account out of harmony with both Mark and Paul, reversing the order of the loaf and the cup.

The case is so complicated that scholarship can never hope to arrive at agreement as to the true text of Luke's account of the Supper. It is altogether possible that those manuscripts which omit verses 19b, 20 represent a harmonistic correction. It is more likely that a scribe would omit the apparently superfluous verse than that he would create a conflict by wedging it in. The original reading was probably a conflation. But whatever may have been the history of the text of Luke's Gospel at this point, it is clearly obvious that we have here two distinct strains of tradition. By placing the three accounts in parallel columns this inference may be impressively exhibited:

9 Thayer, Lexicon, s. v.

Mk. 14:17, 22-25	Lu: 22:14-20	I Co. 11:23-25

And when it came to be morning, he came with the Twelve . . . . And when they had eaten, having taken a loaf, and having blessed it, he broke it and gave it to them and said, "Take: this is my body". *And having taken a cup, having blessed it, he gave it to them, and they all drank of it. And he said to them, "This is my blood of the covenant which was poured out in behalf of many. Indeed, I say to you that no more do I drink of the fruit of the vine until that day when I am drinking it new in the kingdom of God".*

And when the hour came, he sat down, and the apostles with him. And he said to them, "With desire I desired to eat this Passover with you before I suffer; for I say to you that no more do I eat it until it is fulfilled in the kingdom of God". *And having received a cup, having blessed it, he said, "Take this and divide it among yourselves: for I say to you, I do not drink hereafter of the fruit of the vine until the kingdom of God come."* And having taken bread, having blessed it, he broke it and gave it to them, saying, "This is my body which was given on behalf of you: this do as my memorial". And the cup, in like

For I received by tradition (παρέλαβον) from the Lord what also as tradition I transmitted (παρέδωκα) to you: That the Lord Jesus on the night in which he was betrayed took bread, and having blessed it, he broke it and said, "This is my body which is for you: this do as my memorial". And in like manner also the cup, after he had sup-

manner, after he had supped, saying, "This cup is the new covenant in my blood, which was poured out on behalf of you".	ped, saying, "This cup is the new covenant in my blood; this do, as often as you drink it, as my memorial".

The two passages in italic type may very plausibly be regarded as from the same traditional source. Hence we have two distinct traditional sources represented here. Mark's account and the extraneous passage in Luke represent one source, while Luke's basal account and Paul's account represent quite another. Hence we may regard Paul as basing his account of the Supper upon a well-established tradition.[10]

This tradition is marked in a striking way by the use in Luke's record (22:14) of the term "apostle". This word occurs but once in Mark and once in Matthew, while we find it appearing 36 times in Luke-Acts and 24 times in Paul's generally accepted epistles. It occurs 4 times in Ephesians and 5 times in the Pastorals. The fact that the officiial function designated by this title was one of the chief issues between Paul and the Judaizers is a forceful suggestion that apostleship was a matter of vital interest in Judean Christianity, for the basal source of opposition to Paul was certainly Jerusalem. A title translated by $ἀπόστολος$ was ascribed to the chief leaders and teachers in the Jerusalem church,[11] and was therefore of

---

10 But per contra, see Macdonald, **Christian Worship in the Primitive Church**, pp. 140-149. Of course it is quite possible that verses 19b, 20 are an interpolation from Paul's account. Cf. Riddle, **The Gospels**, p. 72f.

11 Cf. Gal. 1:17,19; 2:2,6.

vital significance in Judea; doubtless it was little used
in Galilee. It would then be natural for the tradition
originating in Judea to be pervaded by the use of this
term, while it would be rare in Galilean tradition. The
paramount interest which the title possesses in the Lucan
tradition is signified by Luke's explanatory clause in his
record of the appointment of the Twelve, "whom also he
named apostles" (Lu. 6:13). Comparison with Mark's
account (3:13ff.) shows this clause to be an insertion
into the original tradition. This argues forcibly that it
was a matter of later distinctive community interest.

With language strikingly similar to that which he
begins his account of the Lord's Supper, Paul introduces
his summary of the Passion and Resurrection in I Co.
15:3. "The tradition which I transmitted to you in
your catechumenal instruction (ἐν πρώτοις: rudimentary
instructions) was that which I received." There was a
fixed tradition of the Passion and Resurrection which
Paul had "received" (as transmitted from others,
παρέλαβον). He uses here language concerning the "tradition" (παράδοσις) which we know from Galatians he
would never have used relative to his "gospel" (εὐαγ-
γέλιον). He had learned this tradition himself, and had
taught it, or directed others to teach it to the Corinthians.
Paul's account here presents a parallel to Luke in that
he lists first the appearance to Simon Peter (cf. Lu. 24:12,
34). In other respects Luke's account exhibits a much
later development. However, all that Paul indicates here
could belong to Judea.

From both Paul's epistles and Acts we gain the impression that all Paul's early contacts with Palestinian

Christianity were with Judea. He denies emphatically any dependence upon the original disciples for his "gospel" but of necessity accepted their authority for his "tradition". Such a Palestinian tradition used by Paul must have been Judean in origin, since his early contacts were Judean rather than Galilean. (Cf. Gal. 1:18; 2:1; I Thes. 2:14,15; Ac. 9:26; 11:29,30; 15:4.)

The evident connections between Paul's references to the oral tradition and Luke's account are not to be explained primarily by Paul's personal influence over Luke. In any given locality tradition was common property, so that we have no way of forming the supposition that Paul committed to Luke his own distinctive account of the life of Christ. Paul and Luke labored together and used a common tradition from a common source. Paul's Palestinian contacts had been largely if not entirely with Judea; Luke's Passion Narrative was Judean in origin: there are evident contacts between Paul's tradition and the Passion Narrative of the third Gospel; hence we have strong reason for believing that Judean tradition offers here a common source.

Scholars have long ago observed the evidence for two traditions of the Resurrection appearances, one reflecting Galilee and the other Jerusalem.[12] The evidence is just as strong suggesting the inherently plausible hypothesis that there were two Passion Narrative sources, one reproduced in slightly differing form by Matthew and Mark, and the other reproduced by Luke, and later in a more developed and adapted form by John. Or, stated

<hr>

12 Foakes Jackson and Lake, **Beginnings of Christianity**, vol. v, p. 7; Bacon, **Journal of Religion**, vol. xi, pp. 506-516; **The Story of Jesus**, p. 300.

in another way, we may say that there are in our Gospels three Passion Narratives: the Galilean, recorded by Mark and Matthew; the Judean, recorded by Luke; and the Ephesian, recorded by John.[13] We propose, as this treatise progresses, to make this hypothesis constantly more acceptable.

A glance at any harmony of the Gospels will make these conclusions begin to become impressive. Matthew's Passion Narrative quite evidently arose from a source common with that of Mark.[14] This fact is so familar to the student of the Synoptic Gospels that it were gratuitous to do more than call attention to it. To examine one section discloses the phenomenon in concrete form. Taking by way of example the narrative of the Triumphal Entry, we find in Matthew's record 202 words (according to the Westcott and Hort text). But in this passage is to be found one of Matthew's characteristic references to prophecy, which comes from a special source. In this prophetic citation there are 31 words, which leaves in the material parallel to Mark 171 words. Of these there are 61 which are exact reproductions of Mark and 16 substantial parallels, or a total of 77 words in Matthew's account taken over from Mark. When we compare Luke with Mark the results are quite different. Luke has in this story 259 words, of which 55 exactly correspond to Mark and 11 are substantial parallels. That is, about forty percent of Matthew's account corresponds with Mark and only twenty-five percent of Luke's. In order and arrangement of material Matthew follows Mark. Except for his prophetic references, Matthew's material

13   Vincent Taylor, op. cit., p. 55.
14   Vincent Taylor, op. cit., p. 54.

is practically all parallel to Mark's material, while Luke is obviously independent. These phenomena appear throughout the Passion Narrative. In the Synoptic record of the Passion there are 37 sections.[15] In 27 of these sections Matthew is parallel to Mark, while Luke and Mark are parallel in only 21. In 20 sections where all three are parallel, Matthew agrees more closely with Mark than does Luke. Matthew and Mark appear without any parallel in Luke six times, while Mark and Luke have only one common section not found in Matthew.

John has 20 sections in the Passion Narrative,[16] and of these 9 are independent. Then the 11 sections which are parallel to the Synoptics are but barely substantial in their agreement.[17] It is here to be remembered that it is just in the record of the Passion that John has by far the greatest part of his material which is parallel to the other three Gospels.

These facts have been long familiar in the study of the Gospels,[18] and point forcefully to the conclusion that three traditional sources were in the background of the Gospel record. Proceeding from this evident conclusion we propose that Mark, λ and M were primarily Galilean, while L and π were Judean. That is, our Matthew and Mark were based chiefly upon Galilean tradition, Luke upon Galilean and Judean tradition, and John upon Ephesian tradition.

15 Burton and Goodspeed, **Harmony of the Synoptic Gospels**, pp. 198-261.

16 Robertson, **Harmony of the Gospels**, pp. 152-238.

17 Gardner-Smith, **St. John and the Synoptic Gospels**, pp. 56-72.

18 Variety in character and evidence of types in the material of our Gospels was discerned in the early years of the twentieth century by such pioneers as Wrede, Wellhausen, Johannes Weiss, Flinders Petrie, ét al.

Many years ago (October, 1926) Bacon believed he could discern in the sources of the Gospels "three principal strains of evangelic tradition" which he designated as the source of Mark, the source of Q (S) and the Johannine tradition. "Criticism has not yet succeeded", he observed, "in determining the mutual relations of the three, though there is very general acceptance of the idea that the source represented by Q (a source which we may designate S . . .) is older than Mark, and was to some extent employed by this evangelist also". He finds strong evidence of the dependence of John's Gospl upon this ultimate source S, which is the original basis of the Synoptic Gospels. But under this definition even S is inadequate to fully account for the Johannine materials. "Manifestly some elements, such as the Miracle at Cana, came from outside the known cycle." This source "outside the known cycle" was the Ephesian tradition.[19] Bacon was pointing in the same direction when a short time after he concluded relative to the Resurrection Account: "Thus in Mark and Luke we obtain side by side two variant forms of the tradition, one a Galilean tradition, . . . the other a Jerusalem tradition".[20] The same direction is indicated in Streeter's observation that the widely divergent versions which Matthew and Luke give of common material is not excessive license in handling a common parent document, but "is far more likely to be due to the currency of divergent traditions".[21] This treatise seeks to point toward a closer definition of these divergent traditions and their sources.

---

19   **Hibbert Journal**, vol xxv, pp. 117, 129.

20   **The Story of Jesus**, p. 300.

21   **The Four Gospels**, p. xv.

IV

Thus far we have sought to trace our Gospels to their oral sources. The next stage of our inquiry is indicated by the following question: By what occasion and in what form did the original evangelic tradition come into existence? This question throws us back upon largely hypothetical processes, but a hypothetical basis which can be supported by very convincing historical and literary sources of inference. There are three sets of phenomena which provide these sources of inference; namely, the customs of the Jewish synagogue, the functions and activities of the apostolic churches, and the character of the materials presented in our canonical Gospels.

We may properly begin our inquiry by examining the customs prevailing in Jewish synagogue life, for here the early religious life of the first disciples was nurtured and trained. There can be no reasonable question as to the wide and potent influence of the synagogue upon the primitive Palestinian churches, especially as to their forms of worship and principles of community life.[1] The early Jewish Christians did not construe their faith as a new religion, but as the true and authentic fulfillment of the age-long hope of Israel, the really valid Judaism. Hence they would have no incentive for abandoning the forms of religious activity in which Judaism had been trained.

It is therefore evident that we must approach the practices of the synagogue worship as our first important source of light on the use of early Christian tradition.

1 Petrie, op. cit., pp. 33, 34; Scott, The Validity of the Gospel Record, p. 66; Macdonald, Christian Worship in the Primitive Church, p. 3.

Dibelius has discerned the validity of this method where he says, "To understand the categories of popular writings as they developed in the sphere of unliterary people we must inquire into their life and, in our special case, which deals with religious texts, into the customs of their worship."[2] The materials used in synagogue worship may be classed under three forms. The confessions, ritual prayers and benedictions may be characterized under the head of liturgy. Then there was the reading of passages from the Law, and usually from the Prophets, which we may designate simply as Scripture text. The homily which it was the custom to offer in exposition of the Scripture text we may call exhortation.

For the liturgy the early Palestinian disciples doubtless began by using much of the material which they had learned in the synagogue. Indeed, there is no doubt that they continued to participate in the synagogue services to a large extent, until persecution and the natural tendency to pursue their own religion independently caused them entirely to abandon the synagogue.[3] As they drifted farther from the synagogue they would be inclined to devise more their own liturgical materials. These would be based upon reminiscences of the teachings of their Master. Such liturgical material appears in our Gospels in the Beatitudes and the Lord's Prayer.

For Scripture text the Jewish disciples of course employed the Old Testament, for it has ever been regarded by Christianity as a sacred text. However, these primi-

2 Dibelius, From Tradition to Gospel, p. 8.
3 Macdonald, op. cit., p. 58f.

tive disciples placed far more emphasis upon the Prophets than was characteristic of the synagogue, where the Law held the highest place. Especially would they be interested in Messianic Prophecy, and would be inclined to weave in with the prophecy the fulfillment of it. Seldom would they possess an actual scroll of the text, but would be dependent upon passages retained in memory by members of the community. Thus it is clear how there appear in our Gospel record so many brief Old Testament citations with a crisp reference to the fulfillment thereof. They were an integral part of the tradition, developed in the processes of worship.

The synagogue homily (*midhrash*) was reproduced in the Christian sermon (*kerygma*). We distinguish the two here by different words, but doubtless the early Palestinian Christians called their homilies *midrashim* just as the synagogue did. However, in the Christian assemblies the rabbinic comments would be displaced by sayings and incidents from the life of Jesus. In this early Christian preaching much of the evangelic tradition was formulated.

Our present inquiry is affected not only by the form of synagogue worship, but also by the method of synagogue instruction.[4] As is well known by every student of Judaism, the Jewish teachers of Jesus time were not accustomed to write. All didactic materials were transmitted by word of mouth. This led to fixed and familiar teaching traditions, and such rabbinic tradition was the basis of synagogue instruction. Unquestionably the early Christian communities transmitted their teachings after the

---

4 Bultmann offers an interesting group of parallels of Gospel and rabbinic materials. Cf. **Die Geschichte der synoptischen Tradition,** p. 111f.

same manner. In such teaching tradition great care was exercised to guarantee accurate preservation. This was certainly true in the synagogue instruction, and the motive would be more intense for the same policy in Christian instruction.[5] Such a body of didactic tradition among the Chrisians would consist of sayings and discourses of their Lord, with brief sketches of his personal experiences. In this way a didactic tradition would be produced.

The didactic tradition of the synagogue was differentiated into two types, *halakhah* and *haggadhah*.[6] The former consisted of the specific rules of conduct, while the latter embraced practical examples and admonitions. The influence of these forms of Jewish tradition brought into the Christian tradition many brief, aphoristic sayings as a sort of Christian *halakhah*, and narratives of illustrative incidents as haggadic material. Such a saying as, "Judge not that ye be not judged, etc." (Mt. 7:1) may be regarded as Christian *halakhah*, and such an incident as the epileptic Boy (Mk. 9:9-13) as Christian *haggadhah*.

Our second source of inference is from the functions and practices of the early churches. To reconstruct the *Sitz im Leben* of the evangelic tradition it is essential that we should vizualize the pictures of the assemblies in which the first Jewish disciples gathered.[7] This picture we may with fair accuracy construct from two sources.

5 Scott, **Validity of the Gospel Record,** p. 87.

6 Oesterly and Box, **Religion and Worship of the Synagogue,** pp. 77-100.

7 Bultmann observes that "der urchristliche Gemeinde, niederschlaegt, aus ganz bestimmten Lebensauersserungen und Beduerfnissen dieser Gemeinschaft entspringt, die einen bestimmsten. Stil, bestimmte Formen und Gattungen hervortreiben" (**op. cit.,** p. 4); cf. also Richardson, **The Gospels In the Making,** pp. 37-40.

The first and chief source is documentary. Our earliest glimpse of it is in Ac. 2:46, where Luke describes the Jerusalem disciples as engaged in two forms of assembly, (i) in the Temple courts, and (ii) κατ᾽ οἶκον, which is correctly rendered, "from house to house". That is, they not only assembled daily in the courts of the Temple, where they might most appropriately welcome the returning Messiah, but in the homes of those disciples who were fortunate enough to have houses sufficiently large and ample food supplies to entertain a group of their fellow disciples at meals.[8] To the Jew the meal was a sacred occasion of essential religious significance; therefore, when the primitive Christian disciples gathered in a home at meal-time the gathering became a religious assembly. They prayed together and admonished one another (προσκαρτεροῦντες τῇ διδαχῇ . . . καὶ ταῖς προσευχαῖς, 2:41). But what materials would they employ for such prayer and exhortation? To some extent the synagogue traditions would furnish them with the necessary materials. But more and more they would employ what they remembered of the life and teaching of their Master. Thus from the very beginning their own distinctive tradition would begin its formulation.

There is no reason for supposing that this development in the community life of the first disciples would be confined to Jerusalem. The same factors of religious psychology which gave rise to such customs in Jerusalem would be operative throughout the primitive Christian life of Palestine. Hence we may assume that all through Judea and Galilee comparable developments arose. In all Pal-

8 Macdonald, op. cit., pp. 57-61.

estinian Christianity we may vizualize such groups of
disciples, meeting in homes that could accomodate them
and there rehearsing the teachings and deeds of Jesus,
just as the synagogue traditions recounted memories of
the great rabbis of Judaism.

The Jewish Christian missionaries planted the same
customs in the Gentile world. A picture strikingly similar to that in the background of Ac. 2:46 is reflected
in the language ascribed to Paul in Ac. 20:20, "teaching
you in public assembly and from house to house" ($\delta\iota\delta\acute{a}\xi\alpha\iota$
$\dot{\upsilon}\mu\tilde{a}s\ \delta\eta\mu o\sigma\acute{\iota}\alpha\ \kappa\alpha\grave{\iota}\ \kappa\alpha\tau'\ o\acute{\iota}\kappa o\upsilon s$) The teaching $\delta\eta\mu o\sigma\acute{\iota}\alpha$ might
plausibly have been Paul's ministry in "the school of Ty-
rannus", to which reference is made in Ac. 19:9. In addi-
tion to his discourse in this public hall, Paul went from
house to house, where groups of disciples and novitiates
gathered, and there taught, probably in a more formal
way. There is no reason to regard Paul as an innovator
in this custom; on the contrary, strong reason appears for
considering it a general practice. Confirmation in the
known customs of first century life is re-inforced by the
references to churches in various peoples' houses (Rom.
16:5, 23; I Co. 16:19; Philm. 2).[9] This mode of assembly
became so fixed in early Christian life that the erection
of distinct buildings for worship probably did not begin
until Christianity was more than two hundred years old.
In these house assemblies the evangelic tradition was employed, and thereby formulated and preserved. The order
of service observed is probably reflected in I Tim. 4:13,
"Until I come give attention to the public reading of

9 For an instructive presentation of "house churches" in the New
Testament, see Filson in the **Journal of Biblical Literature**, lviii, part ii,
pp. 105-112.

scripture, to exhortation, to teaching". These distinct elements of scripture reading, exhortation and teaching had a large part in determining the form and content of the gospel tradition.

The second source of light upon this picture is inferential. The evidence is abundant in the New Testament that the early Christian disciples were not long tolerated in the synagogue.[10] When excluded from the synagogues they had no place to meet other than the homes of those who could offer them the required facilities for worship. Out of this necessity arose the house-assemblies.

Then we are not to picture the first century Christian disciples as assembled in a spacious auditorium, engaged in a formal program of worship and addressed in a formal discourse by a speaker previously designated and prepared for the occasion. The *kerygma* of the apostolic churches was not the delivery of a formal sermon, but rather the rehearsal of admonitive or didactic tradition. There was no such distinction as we assume today between teaching and preaching: κήρυγμα and διδαχή were used interchangeably in many instances, and the latter occurs in the New Testament nearly twice as often as the former. The extemporaneous and spontaneous undoubtedly had a large place in the services of the apostolic church,[11] though not a spontaneity which invented from fancy, but rehearsed from memory. This picture

10 Mt. 10:17; 23:34; Mk. 13:9; Lu. 12:11; 21:12; Jn. 12:42; 16:2; Ac. 19:9, etc.

11 Macdonald concludes that "in the early worship, held frequently in private houses, the speaking must have been less formal, more intimate and spontaneous" (op. cit., p. 86).

should bear heavily upon any theory we may form as to the origin of the evangelic tradition.

There obviously lies before us now the question as to what functions and functionaries developed in the course of worship and instruction carried on in these house-assemblies. Here we must reason back from facts indicated at a later stage of development. The first definite information we have of such functions and activities is in I Cor. 12:28, where Paul represents the functions of the church as performed by apostoles, prophets, teachers, etc. With this passage we may compare Eph. 4:11, where church functionaries are described as apostles, prophets, evangelists, pastors and teachers. While the leadership functions here indicated came in developments which belonged to the Hellenistic Christian world, they were devised to propagate the teaching which had originated in the primitive Palestinian churches, and were the last factors to affect the form of the teaching before it was compiled into our canonical Gospels.

These apostles were those vested with chief authority, assumed as having come direct from Christ (I Co. 9:1). It was their responsibility and prerogative to safeguard the authentic teaching concerning the life and redemptive message of Jesus (Ac. 1:21,22; 10:29-43), to preserve a valid tradition, and to supervise activities and developments in a way approved by the risen and ascended Messiah, whose return was regarded as imminent. It was natural that leading apostles should dominate such developments in certain localities. In this way it is plausible to understand that in Syria, about Antioch, the Apostle

Matthew was the apostolic leader, and that his name became attached to the tradition preserved there and to the Gospel based largely on that tradition. In the last years of Peter's life he might have supervised the work at Rome, and such relation might have furnished the basis for the tradition of his connection with the Gospel of Mark. The Apostle John might have been the last to lead Ephesian Christianity, and hence the tradition there could have developed into final written form as the "Gospel According to John". Whatever may be considered the strength of these conjectures, at least the evidence is sufficient for us to conclude that the apostles were the chief guardians of the tradition and the chief promoters of its propagation.[12]

The prophets were those who received such a supernatural quickening of their perceptive powers that they could discern future events and spiritual mysteries. That they had any special relation to the predictive portions of the teaching of Jesus there is no evidence. Nither do we know of any objective reason for supposing that their prophetic messages became confused with the predictive word of Jesus.[13] What we can safely conclude is that their activity in the churches is sufficient evidence that apostolic Christianity was vitally interested in such prophetic materials, and could consequently have taken care to preserve accurately the prophetic words of Jesus. That he gave such prophetic messages is beyond reasonable question, unless one is to repudiate utterly the Gospel

12 In opposition to this view see Cadbury, op. cit., p. 106 n.

13 Easton, The Gospel Before the Gospels, p. 93.

representation of him, and ignore the probable reaction upon him of current Jewish conceptions and practices.

The evangelists were those who entered new fields and introduced the Christian message for the first time, presumably under the direction of the apostles. They would employ in such undertakings much tradition concerning the ministry and redemptive experience of Jesus. His past achievements and future purposes in redemption would be the material for the teaching and preaching of the evangelists, as they approached the pagan world with a religion both strange and unique. The Great Eschatological Discourse, the Passion Narrative and the Resurrection Stories would be just the material such missionaries would of necessity use.

The pastors (elders) had the responsibility of supervising local Christian communities, and planning for the regular services of worship. For their worship programs they would naturally use the forms and materials brought to them by the original Christian missionaries. These original missionaries, usually apostles or evangelists, were provided with the traditional materials derived from Palestine and moulded for the needs of Hellenistic Christianity. Hence the Hellenistic congregations would preserve the elements of the evanglic tradition much as it arose under the influence of the synagogue.

We may safely suppose that the teachers were those who prepared the new converts, the "catechumens", for full church membership, and trained other leaders of the church life. It is probable they were numbered among the elders of the church (I Tim. 5:17). They would make constant use of all forms of the didactic tradition, both narrative and discourse. It is safe to believe that they combined and compiled elements of the tradition, and were the first to reduce the tradition to writing. They were the authors of the Gospel Lessons which were the second stage in gospel development. Without doubt we owe much of the present form of our written Gospels to these primitive Christian teachers.

The third set of facts which should govern our approach to the question of the formation of the original gospel tradition is the nature and form of the materials presented in our existing Gospels. The form which stands out most conspicuously upon the face of our Gospel text is the narrative. Our Synoptic Gospels, and as we shall subsequently see, the Fourth Gospel as well, present the aspect of a collection of brief stories concerning the career of Jesus of Nazareth. But upon closer examination we discover that these stories are not all in the same form. Two fairly distinct types present themselves. There are the more elaborate narratives which would be adapted to homiletic usage, employed as illustrations or instances to reinforce the early Christian preaching. Such material would be used by the evangelists, and any others who discoursed before the Christian assemblies. Then there is another variety, in the form of brief character-sketches and settings for important sayings, more fitted for didactic use. These would constitute some of the earliest materials employed by the primitive Christian teachers. Hence we may distinguish first in the form of our Gospel material *hortatory narrative* and *didactic narrative*.[14]

14 Cf. Bultmann's **Apophthegmata** and **Biographische Apophthegmata,** op. cit., pp. 8, 26.

Then there appear the teachings of Jesus. These are frequently in the form of short aphoristic sayings, lodged in the hortatory narratives or providing a climax for the didactic narratives. But frequently the teaching material appears in the form of long discourses, embracing the parables. These discourses appear in blocks of teaching material which originated probably, not as continuous speeches of Jesus, but as compilations made in the course of the formation of tradition. Some of these units of discourse material, such as the Sermon on the Mount and the Parables by the Seaside, were likely used for hortatory purposes in the early Christian preaching. Such material may be classified as *hortatory discourse*. These discourses took their final form in the written Gospels under the editorial hand of the author. Other blocks of teaching, such as the instructions to the Twelve and the Seventy, and the Eschatological Discourse, were used for didactic purposes. Such discourse material composed the content of instruction used by the teachers in the churches, especially in teaching new converts. Hence we may describe this type as *catechumenal instruction*. Another distinctive form presented itself in the combination of narrative with teaching material, where the narrative is used as an introduction to a discourse. The narration may appear in either of the two typical forms, didactic or hortatory narrative, but is linked on to a compend of sayings and expanded into a rather elaborate teaching situation. We may most naturally think of this process as having been employed by the teachers in instructing the new converts or catechumens. Rather than present to them a series of detached narratives and a list of unoriented teachings, they joined the teachings to narrative settings, which they had their own reasons for believing could properly be combined. We may designate this form as *catechumenate expansion*. An instance appears in Mt. 18:1-35. Others will appear in subsequent discussions.

There were historical developments and situations in the ministry of Jesus which required a recounting much more extensive than the brief narratives. Such materials in the nature of the case required more or less continuous narration. Examples are seen in the ministry of John the Baptist and the account of the Temptation. We may describe this form as *historical narration*.[15] We do not mean by this term to pass upon the problem of the actual historical validity of such records, but only to designate the form by the motive and viewpoint which created it. There is no question that the primitive Christian teachers believed their tradition to be the narration of events which had actually occurred, so in their view and purpose the form of tradition was historical narration.

Then we find materials such as the Lord's Prayer and the Beatitudes, the Magnificat and the Benedictus adaptable to liturgical uses. These passages may have been early Christian ritual. In the written Gospels these are arranged in the form of continuous narration by means of introductions and connections devised doubtless out of other fragments of tradition by the writers. These we may call *editorial material*.

Looking thus at the material of our Gospels against

---

15 Cf. Bultmann's Geschichtserzaehlung, *op. cit.*, pp. 260, 297-308.

the background of the synagogue and the functions of
early church life we may classify them under nine distinct forms: hortatory narrative, didactic narrative, hortatory discourse, catechumenal instruction, catechumenate
expansion, historical narration, liturgy, Scripture text, and
editorial.

It is not within the scope of this dissertation to give
detailed consideration to the text of the Synoptic Gospels,
but close examination will demonstrate this analysis of
form, and it has its specific factor of control in the objective phenomena of synagogue and church life. Such
terms as "legend" and "myth" and "miracle-story" and
"paradigm" are based upon the subjective reactions of
the modern critic rather than the factors of first century
Palestinian church life. Certainly to those first disciples,
pursuing their earnest religious practices, these elements
of tradition did not appear as legends and myths and
miracle-stories and paradigms, but as authentic traditional
materials to be employed as valid elements of worship
and instruction.[16] The scientific method of analysis is
to distinguish the forms by means of the factors operating
in their lives and not the problems which their records
have created in our lives. That there is variety in form
was long ago detected;[17] without question this variety
must have found its cause in the life and customs of the
primitive churches. "Those who told or wrote about Jesus
and the apostles were not imitating literary models, but
were following the natural trend of motives and purposes
which influenced the material."[18]

16 Dibelius, op. cit., p. 26.
17 Petrie, op. cit., pp. 3, 4; especially pp. 33, 34.
18 Cadbury, op. cit., p. 49.

While the scope of our investigation obviates an exhaustive application of our hypothesis to the entire Synoptic record, by way of illustration we may apply it to the first seven chapters of Mark. The opening verse is obviously editorial, and could well have been a customary formula for introducing written reports of evangelic tradition. Then follows a typical Scripture text, a citation of prophecy. It is highly significant as illustrating traditional processes. A passage from the fourth chapter of Isaiah had become familiar in Christian circles because it offered such a satisfactory predicate for an explanation of the relation of John the Baptist to Jesus. The traditional introduction came to be, "Even as it is written in Isaiah the prophet". Later a similar reference was noted in Malachi, which served the same purpose with equal effectiveness. It was therefore combined with the citation from Isaiah, but, according to the tendency of fixed tradition, the introductory clause remained unchanged. Neither the motives nor facilities existed for checking the reference to discover the inaccuracy, so it remained in the tradition and became crystalized in this form. Mark simply selected the obviously appropriate pericope of Scripture text for the introduction to his Gospel, inserting it in its familiar traditional form. He was either ignorant of or indifferent to the fact that the introductory clause mentioned only Isaiah while the citation included also a passage from Malachi. Later scribes in copying the text of Mark took care to correct it, but Mark inserted it just as it was familiar in tradition. The account of the ministry of John the Baptist which follows was doubtless the traditional *midhrash* or comment upon the Scripture text.

At 1:22 appears Mark's most familiar editorial device, his much favored καὶ εὐθύs. With this link he binds together many sections of his Gospel. Here he introduces a brief pericope of didactic narrative, his two-verse account of the Temptation. It is the first of a remarkable chain of didactic narratives, embracing what we have as chapter 1, verses 12 to 45. A glance through these brief paragraphs will disclose their distinct and common character. Each has its brief introductory setting, consisting of an occasion in the Master's experience. "And straightway the Spirit driveth him forth into the wilderness" (v. 12); "Now after John was delivered up" (v. 14); "And passing along by the sea of Galilee" (v. 16); "And they go to Capernaum" (v. 21); "And straightway, when they were come out of the synagogue" (v. 29); "And at even, when the sun did set" (v. 32); "And in the morning, a great while before day" (v. 35); "And there cometh up to him a leper" (v. 40). This but presents the typical form of narrative introduction, true of all traditional developments among all peoples. We begin our stories substantially the same way; for example, "One evening about sunset" . . . "One morning, quite a while before day" . . . "Once upon a time there came to him a leper", etc.

After the introductory setting of time, place or circumstances there follows in these brief narratives the presentation of the issue: some point of controversial or propaganda interest to the early Christian community. For instance, in the narrative in Mk. 1:21-28 the issue is the fact of the demoniac confronting Jesus on a sabbath day. We know from other sources that the sabbath question was a moot point in the life of the primitive churches (Rm. 14:5,6). After the issue is presented, there follows a very succint development of the narrative, which reaches its climax in a profound impression made by Jesus, as in Mk. 1:27,28, or some emphatic pronouncement of truth, as in Mk. 1:38.[19] Thus the typical narrative unit of apostolic tradition presented as its characteristic features setting, issue, development and climax.

In Gospel criticism we call such a unit of tradition a *pericope*. Then a pericope may be defined as a distinct and characteristically formed segment of tradition. The connecting of these pericopae in the form of a continuous narrative may usually be regarded as a literary device of the author. Such we may consider to be the case in the passage before us in Mark. That the incidents occurred in just this consecutive chronological order was not necessarily meant by the author. In fact, in some instances he probably found the material in just this form in tradition, or in some brief Gospel Lesson. Our literary practices would place it under some such caption as, "A Busy Day in Capernaum", but ancient literary customs did not call for captions, nor for chronological sequences. It cannot be too much emphasized that the apostolic tradition of Jesus was never in the least biographical in design. It was wholly didactic and hortatory.[20]

19 It is because of the last mentioned trait of these narratives that Vincent Taylor (op. cit.) calls them "Pronouncement Stories".

20 Dibelius, op. cit., p. 26; Richardson, op. cit., pp. 45, 46; especially Cadbury, op. cit., chapt. x.

In 2:1-12 is a splendid example of hortatory narrative. It has the same typical form of narrative introduction. "And when he entered again into Capernaum after some days"—just as we would say, "Once after an absence of several days he came back to Capernaum". But this story is more detailed and elaborate than the group in the first chapter. It is just the sort of narrative which would serve well as a sermon illustration, and likely originated as an element of apostolic preaching. But this hortatory narrative is followed by another group of didactic narratives. At 3:22-30 we find a pericope of catechumenal instruction. It has the typical pericopate introduction, which may be rendered thus, "Once some scribes that came down from Jerusalem said". With this setting a brief section of teaching is presented.

The material in 4:1-32 presents a clear example of hortatory discourse. It is obvious that parables were especially well adapted to such use. The general statements of 4:33,34 appear to be editorial, then from 4:35 to 5:43 is an assemblage of hortatory narratives. In 6:1-6a we clearly have another didactic narrative, while 6:6b is an editorial connective, followed in 6:7-13 by another didactic narrative. Quite obviously 6:14-29 is hortatory narrative. Verses 30 and 31 appear to be again an editorial connective, followed through the remainder of the sixth chapter by hortatory narrative.

In 7:1-23 we have an excellent example of what we have defined as "catechumenate expansion". If we take only verses 1, 2, 5, 6, we have a quite typical pericope of didactic narrative. Verses 3 and 4 are an inserted editorial explanation. Then the brief pronouncement which constitutes the cimax of the narrative pericope is used as a theme which is elaborated into a considerable discourse. This is a vivid suggestion of the methods of the primitive Christian teacher. This section is followed by two hortatory narratives, woven into the progress of the Gospel story by brief editorial connections which here take the form of chronological sequence.

Such an analysis of form could be pursued throughout the Synoptic Gospels, in demonstration of the fact that the classification we have proposed, defined by the facts and customs of apostolic life, offers a basis of analysis by form of all the material in the Synoptic record. Then we have here an important predicate for testing the source relations of the Fourth Gospel.

V

Our next inquiry is, Have we sufficient reason for concluding that the Fourth Goscpel originated in a manner different from the Synoptic Gospels, or should we apply to the Fourth Gospel the same canons of criticism used with the Synoptics? This raises the converse question, Why should it escape them?

Formerly the Fourth Gospel was consigned to a distinct classification on the supposition that it was doctrinal in character while the Synoptics were historical. But critical research of the past quarter century has largely diminished this differentiation. It is now recognized that all four Gospels are essentially interpretations of Jesus, and hence represent intense doctrinal interests. From 1850 to 1920 it was axiomatic in New Testament criticism to present Mark as the Gospel of distinct historical character. But we recognize now that even Mark is not primarily concerned with history, but with a certain view of the person and experience of Christ. The time is past when Gospel criticism can set John over against the Synoptists in rigid contrast at this point. We are now aware that John only presents here in a more pronounced degree that which is also true of the other evangelists. All four Gospels rest upon the same basal fact in the mind of apostolic Christianity: the tendency to place in permanent form what was believed and taught about Jesus. This consideration brings into a new perspective the whole question of the origin of the Fourth Gospel. Tradition has given us some romantic stories regarding its origin—the less dependable where the more romantic. Conservative criticism has contended that the Gospel originated from the supernaturally quickened and directed memory of the Apostle John. Liberal criticism has devised various theories of a more or less fanciful invention of an interpretative life of Christ by a speculative genius in the early Gnostic Christian circles. Neither of these three methods of approach has been able to throw satisfactory light upon the problem. We are here venturing to point a new method of approach.[1]

Criticism may become "traditional" as well as orthodoxy. It has become a crystalized tradition in New Testament criticism to assume that the Fourth Gospel developed in a way wholly different from the Synoptics. It is a traditional assumption more than the result of careful investigation which causes Dibelius to declare with finality, "In presenting a research in the history of the Form of the Gospels, we must concern ourselves first of all and most of all with only one section of primitive Christian literature, namely the synoptic Gospels",[2] or so cautious a critic as F. C. Grant summarily to conclude that the Fourth Gospel "in no way belongs in the same category with the Synoptists".[3] We believe it possible to demonstrate that in much of the mode of its origin the Gospel of John does precisely belong in the same category with

1 As far as we are aware, represented at the present by only the work of two other men, the British scholar P. Gardner-Smith in St. John and the Synoptic Gospels (Cambridge, 1938), and the German scholar H. Windisch in Johannes und die Synoptiker (Leipsig, 1926), and a few contributed articles. Cf. Howard, The Fourth Gos. In Recent Crit., pp. 85-88.

2 Op. cit., p. 2. However, Dibelius recognizes evidence of John's use of tradition in an article, "The Structure and Literary Character of the Gospels", in the Harvard Theol. Review, xx, pp. 168-170.

3 Grant, Growth of the Gospels, p. 30; cf. also Scott, Validity of the Gospel Record p. 9.

the Synoptic Gospels. Form in the Fourth Gospel and the Synoptics is essentially the same, and this points insistently to similarity in origin.

Recognition of this fact has frequently appeared in recent Gospel criticism, beginning at least twenty years ago, when V. H. Stanton observed "the effects of a period of oral teaching both on the teacher himself who became the author of the Fourth Gospel, and on the form and character of the material which stood ready for his use when he began to compose it".[4] Vincent Taylor believes that in the Fourth Gospel we have not so much the work of the author as the product of the Christian community which he represented. The form of the materials which he employed owed much to processes which were already familiar to his readers by reason of a long period of use. In the opinion of Taylor, while the Gospel is "the work of the Evangelist", it is also "the tradition of Ephesus, the form of the Gospel Story which met its needs, answered its questions, and informed its Christianity". He further registers his conviction that "the existence of a special Johannine tradition is suggested by many points which are peculiar to the Fourth Gospel", and that Ephesus had a Passion Narrative of its own.[5] A tradiitional basis for the Fourth Gospel is recognized by E. F. Scott, one of the greatest living authorities on this book of our New Testament.[6] Lightfoot, while regarding the primi-

---

4 The Gospels as Historical Documents, vol. iii, p. 50.

5 Op. Cit., pp. 53, 54, 188.

6 Op. cit., p. 48. More than thirty years ago Scott wrote, "Granted that the Gospel was written in the first decade of the second century, we can easily conceive that many authentic traditions of the life of Jesus were still extant" He considered that the presence of so much independent material tended to "prove conclusively that the Fourth Gospel

tive tradition as greatly altered by the fourth evangelist, yet is ready to urge that "he is much more strongly influenced by its earlier forms than is sometimes thought".[7] These writers are but recognizing anew what was observed long ago, though with results entirely too negative, by that premier of Johannine critics, Benjamin W. Bacon, now of sacred memory,[8] and are moving with unwitting unanimity toward the conclusion so recently stated by P. Gardner-Smith: "Whoever he was, the author of the Fourth Gospel must have been instructed in the traditions of the Church. It is a fallacy, obvious yet strangely common, to think that he can only have learnt about the life of Christ and the incidents of the ministry from the perusal of some written document".[9]

That the Fourth Gospel is in many respects different from the Synoptics is so obvious that the most superficial student, or the mere novice, cannot fail to observe it. The contention that it is in a different category is in many senses true, but it is a point about which we must be more cautious and discriminating than scholars have usually been in the past. The differences are manifest and familiar to every student of the Gospels.[10] The imperative need

embodies an independent tradition", which caused him to believe that "it is possible that John had sources of information, oral or written, apart from our present Synoptics". (**The Fourth Gospel: Its Purpose and Theology,** pp. 30, 31, 36.)

7 **History and Interpretation In the Gospels,** p. 87.

8 **The Fourth Gospel In Research and Debate,** pp. 28, 29, 88, 153, etc. See also his **Gospel of the Hellenists,** p. 114, and his highly pertinent statement in the **Anglican Theological Review,** vol. xi, p. 203, "The fourth Gospel, like all its predecessors, is built of fragments of older masonry". Cf. Streeter, **The Four Gospels,** pp. 383, 416 ff.

9 **Op. cit.,** p. xi. Cf. Redlich, **An Introducton to the Fourth Gospel,** pp. 110 ff.

10 See especially Scott, **Validity of the Gospel Record,** pp. 49-52. A significant advance in Gospel criticism is marked by the fact that Donald Wayne Riddle in his recent book on the origin and growth of the Gospels

of criticism now is to point out afresh the kindred relations. The Fourth Gospel is different but not alien—it
is in the truest sense a Gospel, reflecting the creative
factors and practical purposes characteristic of Gospel
production.

We believe there exists a strong *a priori* reason for
regarding the Fourth Gospel as a product of tradition,
with a formative history similar to the processes which
resulted in the Synoptic Gospels. Mature reflection leaves
the irresistible conviction that the factors and tendencies
which produced the Synoptic Gospels were operating also
in Ephesian Christianity when the Fourth Gospel arose.
Certainly new converts were being taught so the churches
still had to have teachers. These teachers of necessity
must have material to teach, and we could not suppose
otherwise than that their chief teaching material would
be knowledge of the life and teachings of Jesus. Sermons
were being preached, and hortatory narrative and discourse ascribed to Jesus would still be the most effective
material the preacher could use. Christian worship would
still be using, modifying and developing liturgical material
based on the traditions concerning Jesus. Unquestionably
interest in the earthly career of Jesus was still a vital
force. Material for such activity and interest still was
provided largely by tradition. What the Fourth Gospel
contains is distinctively such material. We have no reason
to suppose that there had arisen in Christian consciousness
at the end of the first century any demand for a formal
history of the life of Christ, and, if we should assume

embraces in his treatment the Fourth Gospel as well as the Synoptics. **(The
Gospels: Their Origin and Growth,** Chicago, 1939)

such a demand, the Fourth Gospel is certainly far from filling it. It is anything but a biographical account of the career of Jesus.

A further reasonable deduction is that we cannot account for the wide and rapid acceptance of the Fourth Gospel if it had been a freehand creation of a fanciful enthusiast, even though its creator had been an apostle. No impeachment of the Fourth Gospel appears until after the middle of the second century, and then objections were based fundamentally upon doctrinal rather than historical reasons. Recently discovered papyrus fragments suggest that the Gospel was already widely used by the middle of the second century.[9] Its immediate acceptance by Ephesian Christianity seems extremely probable. Those who thus received without question or protest the Fourth Gospel were already familiar with much of the substance of its contents. It bore the essential sanction of accepted tradition, although markedly distinctive tradition, quite different from that recorded in the Synoptic Gospels.

The same principle operated in the background of the

9 C. H. Roberts, An Unpublished Fragment of the Fourth Gospel In the John Rylands Library (Manchester University Press, 1935); Bell and Skeat, Fragments of an Unknown Gospel (London, 1935). Streeter, Burkitt and Dodd agree that the latter group of fragments contain traces of the Fourth Gospel. Both were produced before A. D. 150, the former considerably earlier. (Streeter, Four Gospels, p. viii.) Concerning the former publication Barton comments: "Mr. C. H. Roberts discovered in 1934 a fragment written in a style that attests that the copy was in all probability made before the year 150 A. D. The precious leaf contains on its front only seven lines of writing, and on its back only six, but these lines are a part of the text of St. John's Gospel. . . . written before the year 150 in Egypt" (Archaeology and the Bible, p. 588; 7th ed., 1937). Lake comments concerning the latter: "It is a papyrus of the first half of the second century: a combination of Johannine, Synoptic and unknown material. The Fourth Gospel therefore was read and used as a source in Egypt before 150 A. D." (Introduction to the New Testament, p. 53; Harper, New York, 1937.)

Fourth Gospel which E. F. Scott applies to the Synoptics;
namely, that the apostolic public demanded that the material which appeared in written Gospels must be a faithful
reproduction of the tradition already established and
sanctioned by long use.[10] Why should it have been otherwise? There still existed an accepted oral tradition. The
churches were still deeply interested in the historical career
of Jesus, an interest which belongs to the very essence
of the Christian religion. Had it not been for such an
interest in the earthly life of Christ, John would never
have written, or having written, his Gospel would not
have survived.

The oral tradition still had a place of superior respect. The author of II Peter used it in preference to the
written Gospels.[11] The evidence is strong that Clement
of Rome relied upon oral tradition more than upon the
written Gospels.[12] Ignatius appears at several points to
quote from tradition rather than the Gospel text[13] Then
there is the well known attestation of Papias that, well

10 **Op. cit.,** p. 7.

11 Compare 2 Pt. 1:17,18 with Mk. 9:7 || Mt. 17:5 || Lu. 9:35. It
may be countered that the author of 2 Peter was quoting from memory:
but what he remembered was **not** the text of either Gospel. He remembered what Matthew has conflated with Mark, which creates a strong
presumption that he was not quoting from Matthew, but was citing the
tradition from which Matthew derived part of his record. But **per contra**
see C. H. Dodd, **History and the Gospel,** p. 71. Nevertheless, Dodd finds
reflection of the original evangelic tradition in Paul, Hebrews, 1 Peter and
Acts (op. cit., pp. 64-74).

12 Note especially 1 Clem. 13:2; 46:8. There is material corresponding
to Clement's references in the Gospel text, but the vocabulary and arrangement of his quotations are entirely different from either of the Gospels. He
may be quoting loosely from memory of the Gospel text, but it is far more
probable that he is repeating tradition.

13 It is highly significant that all the reflections of the Synoptic
Gospels in Ignatius suggest Matthew's text, yet no one can examine his
references and feel that he was really intending to quote from Matthew
(Eph. 14:2; Smyrn. 1:1; Polyc. 2:2). It appears far more probable that
he was repeating tradition, and if so it was the same traditional source upon
which Matthew was based. We know that Ignatius was from Antioch.

into the second century when the Synoptic Gospels were a half century old, he did not consider it possible to "profit so much from the written documents as from the testimonies of a living and abiding voice".[14] While it is true that the preference for tradition here expressed by Papias reflects an attitude which belonged to the generation that produced him rather than the generation in which he was writing, yet it unquestionably discloses the survival of this attitude to the middle of the second century. His testimony is quite important in the present investigation, because he labored in the very region where the Fourth Gospel originated. Indeed, "Aristion and John the Elder, disciples of the Lord" could have had much to do with the contents of the Fourth Gospel.

Thus there are strong presumptions in favor of the survival and use of tradition in Ephesian Christianity, and when we look at the other side of the question there fails to appear any serious reason against such a conclusion. Hence we must believe that there was an Ephesian tradition existing at the end of the first century. This strengthens the predicate for the further conclusion that in line with all other Gospel productions the Fourth Gospel is tradition formulated into a written record.[15]

Then we may examine the material of the Gospel itself to inquire whether it gives evidence of an origin similar to the Synoptics. On the surface the Gospel ap-

14   Lightfoot, **Apostolic Fathers**, p. 516

15   Many years ago Stanton anticipated this conclusion in the statement, "But even the Fourth Gospel is to be regarded as a work which arose from the writing down of teaching given in the first instance orally in the Christian assembly." (**Gospels as Historical Documents**, vol. iii, p. 282.)

pears to be but a typical piece of Judaeo-Hellenistic hortatory narrative, devised by the genius of a strong, intellectual mystic as a Christian apologetic. But more intimate scrutiny reveals two kinds of evidence pointing toward an origin similar to the Synoptics. There are (1) the evidence of pericopate formation, and (2) the manifest stratification of tradition.

VI

For more than a generation now New Testament scholarship has been greatly disturbed over the order of the material at certain points in the Fourth Gospel.[1] Strauss's "seamless garment" of a century ago has been in danger of developing some serious rents. Moffatt's transpositions are familiar through his *New Translation of the New Testament* even to the general Christian public, and Macgregor has followed and endorsed his re-arrangements of material in the volume on John of the Moffatt series of commentaries. Bernard in his *Gospel According to St. John* proposes yet more readjustments.[2] Many other scholars have made similar efforts, until it has become almost axiomatic in criticism that many sections of the Fourth Gospel are out of order. Perhaps so: but they are right where the author placed them.

If the writer had been composing with a free hand, and writing as his thought moved on in logical or chronological continuity, we might have had the consistent flow of ideas and connection of events which the modern scholars so earnestly seek; but a writer selecting from tradition a segment here and another yonder, would not find it nearly so easy to preserve the proper sequences, and we cannot assume that he had any conscious purpose which imperatively required such consistent order.

The very fact which so readily facilitates Moffatt's

1 Bacon, **The Fourth Gospel in Research and Debate**, pp. 497ff.

2 Filson, **Origins of the Gospels**, p. 186; see especially Lewis, **Disarrangements of the Fourth Gospel**, the footnote in Bacon, **op. cit.**, p. 498, and Redlich **op. cit.**, pp. 103 ff.

transposition of 3:22-30 to a position following 2:12 is the pericopate character of the section. It begins with an introduction which gives it its own setting of time, place and circumstances. The seemingly awkward representation of Jesus going out of Jerusalem into Judea, when Jerusalem was located in Judea, is sufficiently explained if we understand the introductory phrases as crystalized by tradition and embodied in the Gospel by the writer without thorough revision. The pericope might have begun with some such phraseology as, "Jesus and his disciples came into the land of Judea", with no previous reference to Jerusalem. It is a typical pericope of didactic narrative, presenting its point of special interest, which was controversy over John the Baptist's official qualifications. It presents a brief development and reaches a climax with an important saying, an emphatic testimony of John to Jesus. There could not be a more typical pericope from tradition. It suits Dr. Moffatt better following 2:12: it suited the writer better where he had it. He was not composing a literary document but making a record of tradition—undoubtedly using a high degree of editorial freedom in doing so, but nevertheless recording tradition. The apparent displacements of tradition are points where the author failed to follow faithfully our standards of rhetorical sequence and historical continuity. A better understanding of the origin of the Gospel will bring a better understanding of this phenomenon.[3]

That the fact of pericopate formation in the Fourth Gospel has already begun to dawn upon the mind of Gospel criticism is seen in such statements as that of

3 Bacon, op. cit. p. 526f.

Dibelius: "The consciousness that his book contains a selection of narratives is not altogether lacking in the author of the Fourth Gospel"; and in a footnote Dibelius calls attention to concrete evidence with an analogy from Hellenistic literature.[4] Especially does he find specific pericopae of the type which he calls "tales".[5] Vincent Taylor discerns evidences of pericopate formation in at least two passages.[6]

Our test of pericopate formation in the Fourth Gospel may begin with that familiar passage universally recognized as a pericope from tradition, 7:53-8:11. It was not in the original text of the Fourth Gospel, and was never a part of that Gospel until more than a hundred years after the Gospel was written. It was a floating pericope, preserved in some way unknown to us, and inserted finally in the text of John. It is typical in its pericopate formation. There is the introduction in the form of a brief setting of time, place and circumstances. An issue of intense community interest is thrust forward in the form of a woman accused of the overt act of adultery. Development of the issue is described, and the climax is reached in the triumph of the compassionate spirit of Jesus over the hypocritical exactions of the Jewish officials. For many generations it survived in Christian circles as a most impressive example of hortatory narrative. It fulfills this form as perfectly as any section which could be found in all the Gospel of Mark, or anywhere else in

4 Op. cit., p. 40; cf. also Harvard Theol. Review, xx, pp. 168-170.

5 Ibid, pp. 71, 91.

6 Formation of the Gospel Tradition, p. 82f. Quite a thorough treatment of this aspect of the Fourth Gospel has been offered by H. Windisch in Gunkel, Eucharisterion, Book ii, pp. 174-213.

the Synoptic record. Though not an original part of the Fourth Gospel, it provides a typical example with which to compare other form elements in the book in testing the degree of its pericopate formation.

We may turn now to three original sections of the Fourth Gospel whose pericopate formation is established in advance. These are the three parallels to the Synoptic Gospels which appear in John's record of the ministry: the Cleansing of the Temple (2:13-22), the Miracle of Feeding (6:1-15), and the Triumphal Entry (12:12-19). These records differ in connection, wording and details from the Synoptics, but in *form* they are exactly parallel. Each is a thoroughly integrated story within itself, that can be told intelligently independent of its context. Form critics are unanimously agreed that the three accounts as they appear in the Synoptic record, are distinct pericopae of tradition, so at least the form is already accepted for the Fourth Gospel.

We now have before us four sections of the present text of the Fourth Gospel which are established by other related facts as pericopae. When we compare them with other parts of the Gospel of John there is nothing extraneous or unique in their character nor in the way in which they are incorporated into the Gospel. Much else in the Gospel is quite similar in form. We may take for instance the Cleansing of the Temple (2:13-22) and compare it with the section right by it, the Miracle at the Wedding Feast (2:1-11). The pericopate formation of both sections is along precisely the same lines, with setting, issue, development and climax, and since the

Cleansing of the Temple is so closely parallel in form to the Synoptic account of the same event we have the narrative of the Miracle at the Wedding Feast in an exact juxtaposition to characteristic pericopate formation in the Synoptic tradition.

And Dr. Moffatt has done us the favor of lodging another very typical pericope right in the same connection, for, as already observed, he places 3:22-30 following 2:12. We have noted the distinct pericopate character of this section. It is a typical piece of didactic narrative. It is not a story told for interest or inspiration, but an example adduced for instruction. But it presents the characteristic setting, issue, development and climax of the narrative pericope, just as clearly as the Synoptic parallel which Dr. Moffatt has placed immediately following it.

When we turn to John's Synoptic parallel at 6:1-15 we again find a similar formation in close proximity. The Healing of the Lame Man is at the beginning of the preceding chapter (5:1-9). If on one side of John's account of the Miracle of Feeding one will place the Synoptic record of the same incident, and on the other the section which narrates the Healing of the Lame Man, we can detect no essential differences in form. It is a typical piece of hortatory narrative. A Jewish festival at Jerusalem, with the invalids gathered about the pool of Bethesda, provides the background of time, place and circumstances. One particular invalid, afflicted for thirty-eight years, becomes the point of special interest in the story. The point of interest is developed by means of a brief dialogue between the lame man and Jesus. The climax is in the complete healing of the man: "And immediately the man got to be well, and took up his bed and began walking about" (verse 9). In form we have precisely the same phenomena of story development that appear in Mark's account of the Healing of the Paralytic (2:1-12).

The record of the Triumphal Entry (12:12-19), with its Synoptic parallel on one side, has just over against it on the other side a literary unit of exactly the same form (12:1-8). The setting, the issue or point of interest, the development, the climax, are all there, just as you would find them in any distinct story from the Gospel of Mark. It is typical didactic narrative, culminating in a saying of Jesus in the precise form of Vincent Taylor's "Pronouncement Story". Then immediately following the record of the Triumphal Entry is another striking pericope of didactic narrative. The story of the inquiring Greeks is used to introduce a unit of teaching. The section taken as a whole (12:20-36) presents a typical case of catechumenate expansion, closely similar in form to the example cited above in Mark (7:1-23). The form and limits of the didactic material in John's Gospel is a problem we deal with later.

Now with the array of these proven pericopae before us, there will be felt no hesitancy in adding another, the Healing of the Man Born Blind (9:1-7). When we contemplate just the first seven verses of the ninth chapter, we have a very clear pericope of hortatory narrative. The use

of it for controversial setting is a further and a later development, which is to be discussed in the sequel.

Thus by comparison of John's Synoptic parallels with
the other sections of his Gospel we discern what is unquestionably pericopate formation. The question now
arises, Whence did John derive these pericopae? He obtained none of them from the Synoptic Gospels, because
while the form is parallel, the connection, style, wording,
and much of the content differ.[7] We are unable to posit
any other written source as a possibility. The only plausible conclusion left us is that he derived these pericopae
from a stream of tradition separate from the Synoptic
tradition, yet having somewhere important points of
contact.

This hypothesis of pericopate formation offers interesting solutions to some problems of interpretation in the
Fourth Gospel. The regulatory effect of the Fourth
Gospel on the chronology of the life of Christ vanishes
with a thorough application of this theory. In Jn. 2:13
there is a reference to a Passover, and again in verse
23 of the same chapter, the next paragraph, there is a
reference to Passover. Is it the same Passover? Surely
not. It is a seriously strained position to disregard the
great weight of the Synoptic testimony by placing the
Cleansing of the Temple at the beginning of the ministry
of Jesus in deference to John alone. And if John was
using pericopae from tradition, he had no intention of
making the references to the Passover data for chronology. The reference to the Passover is merely a part of

7 Gardner-Smith, op. cit., pp. 88-97.

the introduction to the pericope, and is about as we should say, "Once at Passover-time Jesus did thus-and-so". Hence John was not arranging his material to fall in a certain definite period of time between three or four Passovers. Had he been, he would have designated more particularly the feast mentioned in 5:1. It is so very obvious that we meet at this point, not the historian's chronological datum, which certainly would have designated the feast, but the story-teller's devise of introduction, "After this, once at a Jewish feast-time Jesus went up to Jerusalem". Which feast was an immaterial point in processes of oral tradition. John's Gospel can never settle the chronology of the life of Christ.

Other problems of lesser magnitude come into clearer light with the assumption of this pericopate hypothesis. For instance, at 6:1 appears a difficulty which has baffled expositors from the days of Tatian to the present. At the close of chapter five Jesus is in Jerusalem. Then abruptly chapter six begins, "After these things Jesus went away beyond the Sea of Galilee (or Tiberias)". Went away from where? Had he been in Galilee this form of expression would have been immediately intelligible, but as connected with previous activity in Jerusalem it is startlingly awkward. Beginning as far back as Tatian, the effort has been made to straighten out the connection by transposing the fifth chapter to a position following the sixth, and thereby bringing in the sixth chapter immediately after the Healing of the Nobleman's Son at Cana of Galilee.[8] This is manifestly a violent pro-

8 Bacon, op. cit., p. 506.

cedure, but seems to be the only solution until we begin
to contemplate the Gospel as a compilation from tradition.
In the pericope as formulated in tradition this form of
introduction was used, and John inserted it without alter-
ing the phraseology. It originated in the usual way of
starting a story, "Once he went over on the other side
of the Sea of Galilee", having in mind that most of the
Galilean ministry was on the western side of the lake, the
distinctively Jewish side. As an introduction of a pericope of tradition it is natural; as connectional phrasing
in continuous historical composition it would be quite con-
fusing.

At 6:8 the Greek student is bewildered to find Andrew
presented as, "One named Andrew, the brother of Simon
Peter", as though mentioned for the first time. ('Ανδρέας ὁ
ἀδελφὸς Σίμωνος Πέτρου — note absence of article from
'Ανδρέας.) But Andrew has been most impressively introduced at 1:40, and his relation to Simon Peter indicated
there; so the Greek student would expect that any subsequent reference to him would be as ὁ 'Ανδρέας — "the
Andrew" already made known. But the Miracle of Feeding was a popular and much used story, as attested by
its six appearances in the fourfold Gospel record and its
presence in all three strains of evangelic tradition, Galilean,
Judean and Ephesian. In tradition it was told independent
of any context. Hence Andrew was customarily identified
in the story by his relation to his far better known brother
Simon, and for that purpose the Greek as John has it here
is in exactly the properly adapted form. He simply wrote
it in as it was already familiar in the tradition, and with-

out special view to the fact that Andrew had already
received an elaborate introduction earlier in the book.

At 7:1 there is a strange passage. It is quite broadly
summary in its nature, and is difficult to place in any
scheme of the life of Christ based upon the Synoptic
record. Literally rendered it reads, "After these things
Jesus began going about in Galilee, for he came to the
point that he was not willing to continue going about in
Judea, because the Jews were seeking to kill him". Such
a rendering is necessary to bring out the present and
imperfect tenses of this passage, and yet it presents a
picture of a definite period of activity in the ministry of
Jesus. It seems to imply that Jesus has not been in Galilee
before. Furthermore, its location just at this point in
John's record raises difficulties in comparison with the
Synoptic record. If the Feast of Tabernacles mentioned
in the next verse was the last Feast of Tabernacles before the crucifixion, and undoubtedly it was, since it discloses the Jewish opposition at the saturation point, then
according to the Synoptic representation Jesus was very
cautious in moving about Galilee at this period, and was
on the point of departing from Galilee for Judea for the
very reason that this verse has him coming into Galilee
from Judea. The passage is in embarrassing conflict with
the Synoptic record as a description of a policy of Jesus
immediately preceding his final departure from Galilee, but
it is quite appropriate as an epitome of the entire Galilean
ministry. In fact, such we believe it to be. We would
explain it as a brief pericope of Judean tradition used to
summarize the Galilean ministry. The Feast of Taber-

nacles which John next describes closed the Galilean ministry, consequently he employs this bit of traditional summary as an introduction. Several such traditional summaries may be found in the Synoptic record.[9]

It is interesting to note that in the introduction to the account of the Raising of Lazarus (11:1,2) there is a reference to the Anointing at Bethany, and in the introduction to the record of the Annointing at Bethany there is reference to the Raising of Lazarus. Now for free composition of continuous historical record this would be rather strange, but it is perfectly natural for two stories current in tradition. John recorded them as he had many times told them in oral discourse, and as he had heard them told.

In 14:31 the record reports Jesus as saying, "Arise, let us go hence", as though he is bringing his discourse to a close; yet the discourse goes right on for two more chapters. The traditional explanation has been that Jesus at this point left the room where he had partaken of the Last Supper and delivered to the disciples the remainder of the discourse as they walked on toward Gethsemane. Critical interpretation has offered various explanations, the favorite one being a re-arrangement of material. If chapters 14 to 16 be recognized as a compilation of several discourse pericopae from tradition the difficulty disappears. One traditional discourse which the evangelist selected closed at this point, and he retained the exact wording of the tradition, though he went on to add other discourse material. This explanation will also take care of the prob-

9 For instance Mk. 1:14,15,39; Mt. 4:23-25; 9:35; Lu. 4:44; 21:37.

lem observed by Bacon that, "There is cearly a great deal in Jn. 15-16 which only re-echoes ideas expressed in Jn. 13-14".[10] The evangelist has combined more than one discourse preserved in tradition, since he knew all of them to belong to the close of the ministry. Bacon's original Author and Redactor now become Ephesian tradition and author—surely a more plausible hypothesis.

Thus far we have certainly established for our hypothesis of pericopate formation a predicate of strong probability. We may now proceed to apply it to the structure of the Gospel in detail. There are phenomena in the Prologue, already recognized by the most competent scholarship,[11] which establish beyond reasonable doubt the traditional origin of that portion. Lodged in this section are what appear to be the stanzas of an ancient hymn (1:1-5, 10-12, 14, 16-18), the rhythmical nature of which is obvious to the novice. Such hymn or hymns must have been used in the Asian congregations for liturgical purposes. Just as a writer today freely quotes such liturgical material, so John uses this hymn of his time as the chief substance of his introduction.

Into the ancient hymn John has interpolated a brief descriptive statement concerning the origin and purpose of the Baptist. It may be observed that by reading continuously through verses 6 to 8 and 15 we have a brief summary statement of the relation of John the Baptist to Jesus.

10　**Gospel of the Hellenists,** p. 137.

11　Bacon, **Gospel of the Hellenists,** pp. 243ff.; 311-314; Grant, **Growth of the Gospels,** pp. 220-223; Colwell, **John Defends the Gospel,** p. 128; Bultmann, "Der religionsgeschichtliche Hintergrund des prologs zum Johannes-Evangelium" in Gunkel, **op. cit.,** pp. 3, 4.

There appeared a man, sent from God, whose name was John. That man was for a witness, that he might witness concerning the Light, that all might believe through him. That man was not himself the Light, but was designed to bear witness for the Light. John bears witness concerning him and cried saying, "This was the one concerning whom I said, 'The one coming after me has taken precedence over me, because he was superior to me' ".

One immediately observes the characteristic form of didactic narrative, especially defined by its climax in an important saying. It could easily and effectively have served as a pericope of elementary instruction in the churches. Hence it appears plausible to suppose that the Prologue to the Fourth Gospel consists of the interweaving of an ancient hymn and a pericope of didactic narrative from catechumenate instruction.

We may look now at the great body of the Gospel as it lies before us. As to analysis, we begin by accepting the observation of so many able commentators that there are two main divisions, a manifestation of the divine Logos-Messiah to Israel through chapter 12, and a manifestation to the Twelve through chapter 17.[12] The section embraced in chapters 18 to 20 is obviously distinct, and it is all but a settled conclusion now that chapter 21 is an appendix, with verses 24, 25 a postscript.

Various bases have been adopted for the study of the structure of the Fourth Gospel. The traditional method was to seek to place it side by side with the Synoptics in a chronological scheme; then others insisted

12 Thus Paul Feine (**Einleitung in das Neue Testament**, p. 91) says: "Es gliedert sich in zwei Hauptteile 1. das Wirken Jesu in der Welt 1:19-12:50, 2. seine Rueckkher zum Vater 13:1-20:29".

that the author's plan was logical, and in no sense involved chronological sequence; and still others maintained that his design was dramatic; while a despairing residue have categorically denied that he had any plan at all. A beautiful scheme of late has reconstructed the book around the sacred number seven. It is not the purpose here to dispute or endorse any of these methods of analysis—doubtless they all have their merits. We would emphatically call attention, however, to a phenomenon in the structure of the Gospel which we all have overlooked. It is laid out in five large blocks of material, distinguished by the character of the material composing each block. Only a glance discloses this fact.

The first block of material embraces 1:18-4:54. It is chiefly narrative, consisting of a series of stories concerning Jesus, strung together in rather loosely connected fashion, with one considerable piece of discourse in the midst (3:3-36). We have here a sort of miniature Mark. The pericopate formation is pronounced and distinct. There are in this block of Gospel material ten clearly marked pericopae, connected by brief sections of editorial material or fragments from tradition.[13]

The section 1:19-27 begins with the most typical pericopate formation. There is an introductory generalization ("and this is the witness of John") and definition of occasion("when the Jerusalem Jews sent priests and Levites to him"). Then the section presents in a succinct and comprehensive way an important issue of community interest, the true character and mission of John the Baptist.

13 Jn. 1:19-27. 29-34, 35-42, 43-51; 2:1-10, 13-21; 3:1-8, 22-30; 4:1-42, 46-53.

It is developed in the form of a dialogue between John and the Jerusalem delegation and reaches its climax in John's summary confession of his inferiority to Jesus. It is a perfect example of didactic narrative, as typical as any pericope anywhere in the Synoptic record. Verse 28 is possibly an editorial explanation of the writer, but we regard it as more probably a community explanation added at a later stage in the development of the pericope.

There follow three sections which John strings together with τῇ ἐπαύριον, which usually is rendered "on the morrow". But the supposition that John meant to be detailing in precise chronological sequence the happenings of a series of consecutive days meets a grave difficulty. On this supposition the third τῇ ἐπαύριον would indicate a fourth day, and the Miracle at the Wedding Feast would mark a fifth day. Yet the writer begins his account of the Wedding Feast with the phrase, "And on the third day" (2:1). Apparently he means to date the Wedding Feast from the preceding incident, at which time Jesus returned to Galilee (1:43). Hence John seems to be using these designations of time, not to establish a rigid list of consecutive dates, but as a convenient linking of his series of stories, just as we would say, "then on a later day". It is a very natural method of connecting pericopae of traditional narration which belong in one general development of events, such as the gathering about Jesus of his earliest disciples.

The three sections composing 1:29-51 bear all the characteristics of didactic narrative. Each is introduced by a brief setting, and each presents its process of development to a climax in a saying of propaganda interest. The first culminates in a testimony of John the Baptist to Jesus, the second in a significant communication of Jesus to Simon Peter, and the third a striking apocalyptic pronouncement. They present precisely the form phenomena of Vincent Taylor's "Pronouncement Stories". The exaltation of Peter and the apocalyptic declaration were not of any distinctive interest in Ephesus at A.D. 100, but there had been stages and localities of apostolic tradition in which both would have possessed intense propaganda interest. While neither saying would have concerned Ephesus at the close of the first century, both would have been of deep interest in Judea about the middle of the first century. The pericope culminating in the testimony of the Baptist held great polemical concern for the evangelist, while for him the second and third pericopae were of interest as affording an account of the gathering of the group of authorized messengers of the divine Christ. Thus we have a phenomenon which is of frequent occurrence in the Synoptic Gospels: materials employed by the evangelist to promote interests different from those which operated in the origin of the tradition.

In 2:1-11 Vincent Taylor recognizes what he terms a "Miracle Story".[14] It is an obvious example of what we have classified as a hortatory narrative. It is a story designed to illustrate the power of Jesus, and would be just the sort of anecdote which would be popular for use in early Christian preaching. We have already observed how obvious is its pericopate formation when compared with the following section (verses 13-22), which is a

14 Op. cit., p. 120.

Synoptic parallel. Verse 11 is clearly an editorial comment, and verse 12 is an editorial connection, probably
formed from a fragment of tradition.

An interesting section confronts us at 2:23-3:21. It
is an instructive case of the developed didactic narrative
just such as we have observed as "catechumenate expansion" in Mk. 7:1ff. At the core of it there is a didactic
narrative, the original typical form of which we may
detect. It is embraced in 3:1-8. There is the brief setting
of time (night), place (Jerusalem, by implication), and
circumstances (a sanhedrist seeking enlightenment from
Jesus). The issue is the new birth. The development is
the dialogue between Jesus and Nicodemus. The climax
is the pronouncement of Jesus upon the necessary mystery
of the new birth. Such the story likely was in its original
form, as it circulated in the churches of Asia. But the new
birth was a doctrine of ever growing import, as the
churches faced the encroachments of pagan thought and
religion, and was indeed an adaptation of the interpretation of Christian experience to certain pagan religious
conceptions; therefore the propagation of the doctrine
became urgent for Christian teachers. We may well
imagine that it was in response to some such need as this
that this brief didactic narrative developed into a discourse. The introduction (2:23-25) is probably editorial,
for it is an interpretation of the reaction of the Jewish
masses which presents decidedly the character of personal
opinion. Whether all the discourse material of 3:10-21
is meant as coming from the lips of Jesus we cannot tell.
There is a rhythm in verses 16-21, and an intense doctrinal
tone which strongly suggests liturgy. These verses may

have been a ritual of confession used in the churches. Or this material could have been catechumenal instruction, appended to the discourse of Jesus. At any rate, when we view the passage as a development from an original brief didactic narrative, it lifts into new perspective the question as to how far the didactic material in the Gospel of John is to be regarded as representing actual teaching of Jesus. We will find this question appearing in a new light throughout the Gospel.

We have treated 3:22-30 in a former connection, and found it a typical pericope of didactic narrative. Verses 31-36 are an editorial insertion. They compose what looks very much like another brief ritual of confession or selection from catechumenal instruction.

There is no part of the Fourth Gospel which presents more vividly its primitive origin and local interest than 4:1-12. It is a little "Samaritan Gospel". Nowhere in the Gospel record is the local coloring more vivid and abundant. The detailed evidences of this fact are too familiar to require rehearsal here. There is scarcely a verse that does not bear directly or indirctly upon the local setting. Mention may be made of the woman coming at noon to draw water, at a time when she could avoid embarrassing contact with the reputable women of the village, who would visit the well in the evening; the surprise of the Samaritan woman that a Jew should so ignore prejudices and conventionalities as to speak to her; and the reference to Gerizim as "this mountain", since it was just above the locality at which the conversation took place. We have here more than a pericope; it is an extensive local tradition which had at an earlier time grown up in the churches of Judea and Samaria, and had somehow been transplanted to Asian soil. How the transplanting took place will be suggested at a later point in this discussion. In form it may be classified as historical narration.

In 4:43-45 we have an editorial connection, based upon a fragment of tradition which will come up for consideration in a subsequent chapter. There follows (4:46-53) a hortatory narrative of perfectly typical form. It almost begins with a familiar "Once upon a time", though here it is "Then again" (vs. 46). This, combined with the mention of Cana and, in doubtless an editorial phrase, the miracle earlier performed there, constitutes a setting. The issue is a severe illness which has befallen a prominent home. The development is the testing of the father's faith, and the climax is the complete restoration of the son, with the resulting faith of the household. The incident is very probably a parallel to the Healing of the Centurion's servant in the Synoptic tradition (Mt. 8:5-17; Lu. 7:1-10), but the radical divergencies of John from the Synoptic record show that his account could not have been derived from the same source. It was the same incident developed into a pericope of two different lines of tradition.[15] Verse 24 is obviously editorial.

Thus the first great block of material in the Fourth Gospel presents a most manifest pericopate formation. Such form points infallibly toward traditional origin. Hence our predicate is yet more securely strengthened for

15 Gardner-Smith, op. cit., pp. 22-24.

assuming an Ephesian tradition.

The next block of material is quite the largest in the book, embracing 5:1-10:39. Probably to the mind of the author it was the heart of his Gospel. It is chiefly composed of discourse material treating various themes which are interwoven into the discourses in such way as to defy systematic analysis. To aggravate the apparent jumbled state of the material, there are several pericopae of narrative material scattered along at intervals.

We discover five of these narrative pericopae, 5:1-9; 6:1-14; 7:2-9; 9:1-7; 10:22-25. Are they scattered at random through the discourse material, with no evident plan of structural function? There is a rational assumption which offers a strong antecedent objection to such a view. It is the high grade of intelligence which the writer everywhere else exhibits. Such intelligence would not degenerate into a slipshod method at the heart of his book. Then when we examine the material closely we find that there is a manifest plan into which the narrative pericopae fit quite logically and effectively. The block contains five distinct controversial discourses, and a narrative pericope is employed as the introduction and background of each.[16] The incident recounted in the narrative pericope furnishes a historical occasion for the controversy, and from it arises an issue between Jesus and the Jews. This issue evokes a discourse, more or less in the form of a debate. This plan is obvious throughout the entire block of material.

16 Bacon, Gospel of the Hellenists, pp. 139ff.

The first controversy is introduced by the Healing of the Lame Man (5:1-9). It is developed as a characteristic pericope of hortatory narrative through verse 9a. Then we witness a process which operated widely in the development of the evangelic tradition. It is what we have called catechumenate expansion. As an auxiliary angle to the story it was known in the early Christian circles that the healing was on the Sabbath day, and was therefore impeached by the Jewish authorities. This enabled Christian teaching to extend a brief pericope of hortatory narrative into a compend of catechumenal instruction. The dialogue thus developed from the pericope our author uses as a definition of the issue in the first controversy. Upon it he bases the discourse, which presents the divine basis of Christ's authority in his unique relation to the Father.[17]

The most bafflling problem which faces us in the entire study is, Whence did the author derive this discourse material? Some would dismiss the question lightly by pronouncing it his own metaphysical speculations put into the mouth of Jesus. But the more cautious critic will not be content with such a light and easy solution. To suppose that it is an exact reproduction of the original Aramaic teaching of Jesus is another extreme conclusion which caution rejects. The style is the same as that in the narrative portions of the Gospel, and quite different from the record of the teaching of Jesus in the Synoptics, which obviates the possibility of the material being a translation

17 It was interesting to find, nearly a year after this paragraph was first written, the observation of Gardner-Smith that in this chapter "the Fourth Evangelist has taken a story familiar in oral tradition, worked it up, and used it for his own purpose". (**Op. cit.,** p. 25.)

of the original Aramaic teaching of Jesus. Yet it is
certainly not a misrepresentation of Jesus — either of his
thought or the spiritual depths of his personality. There
is a clear and irresistable conviction that what we read
here in the Fourth Gospel somehow goes back to Jesus,
though not through exact words from his lips. Nor can
we believe that the author devised these discourses out
of a few wisps of memory or tradition on the spur of the
moment. These things he had preached and taught many
times, and had doubtless led others in preaching and
teaching. It is such material as may be assigned to the
form which we have designated as "hortatory discourse".
It belonged to the *kerygma* of the apostolic church.

Many critics have uncounsciously become obsessed
with the idea that the Fourth Gospel represents the only
public expression from its author and was first delivered
to readers to whom the material was new and strange.
He had never presented it before: they had never heard
it before. On the contrary, one capable of such a product
could only have been a pre-eminent leader of wide influence and long experience.[18] B. H. Streeter regards it
as a safe presumption that the materials which this author
incorporates in his Gospel he "had already used time
after time in discussions with individuals or in addresses
to the church".[19] He had preached and taught long and
acceptably in Ephesian Christianity. What we have in
the Fourth Gospel can most reasonably be thought of as

18 Quite conceivably Bacon's "Ephesian Elder", discussed at length
in his Gospel of the Hellenists.

19 Four Gospels, p. 383. Strikingly similar is Stanton's conclusion:
"But even the Fourth Gospel is to be regarded as a work which arose from
the writing down of teaching given in the first instance orally in the
Christian assembly". (The Gospels as Historical Documents, vol. iii, p. 282.)

the well tried material which the author had gathered
through his long teaching experience. And it was material
familiar and acceptable in the churches. He would be
most naturally inclined to make written record of it as it
became evident that life was drawing toward a close. The
Gospel was likely his last as well as his greatest teaching
achievement.[20]

Then the discourse material used in forming these
controversies is the teaching of Ephesian Christianity
about Jesus, and teaching which was ascribed to Jesus
in the confidence that it was based upon his authority
and Messianic character. Whether it consisted of a
verbatim report of the Master's language is a question
which probably never came within the horizon of their
thinking.

At the beginning of the second controversy we have
a familiar Synoptic parallel in the Miracle of Feeding
(6:1-14). Here we have a case of catechumenate expansion which appears in the Synoptic record also. It is the
appending of the narrative of Stilling the Tempest to
that of the Miracle of Feeding. John inserts a verse of
editorial explanation between the two narratives, but
otherwise he developes the entire story about as Matthew
and Mark do. Luke has the Miracle of Feeding, but not
the Stilling of the Tempest. The narrative of the Stilling
of the Tempest is not in the characteristic pericope
formation. It undoubtedly originated as an appendage to

20 Bacon thinks of him as "most certainly a veteran", and cites very
convincing evidence from the Johannine Epistles, undoubtedly by the same
author as the Gospel. (Gos. of the Hellenists, p. 56.) To Streeter the
Gospel is "an old man's farewell" (op. cit., p. 465.)

the other story. The combined narrative serves John as the historical occasion for his second controversy. The issue appears when Jesus addresses the gathered throngs in the synagogue at Capernaum, and consists of the question as to the real design and character of the Messianic mission. The discourse, again somewhat in the form of a debate, follows. An editorial climax is added as the culmination of the incident. This conclusion is not in pericopate formation, but may nevertheless be a selection from tradition.

The significant character of 7:1 we have discussed above. Then follows a narrative of rather distinct pericopate formation. It may have been selected from a considerable tradition which developed out of the relation of Jesus to his family, and would most likely have been formulated in Judea, where the family of Jesus abode after the Resurrection and where they were influential in Christian circles. A brief tradition of the same tone and setting recorded in Mark (3:31-35) would be a Galilean fragment of the same tradition. The tradition before us here serves our author as an introduction to his third controversy. It constitutes a brief historical setting but in no way gives rise to the issue which the controversy develops. The issue arises when Jesus finally reaches the Feast of Tabernacles. It concerns the source of Jesus' teaching. The discourse which follows is composed of a great aggregation of teaching related more or less intimately to the general idea of Jesus' Messiahship. Dialogue and incident are deftly interwoven into the discourse. Unless one takes the position that the writer is devising a piece of pure fiction, then we must suppose that he has gathered a group of traditions which he had reason to believe were connected with the experiences and utterances of Jesus at the last Feast of Tabernacles which he attended. Certainly the material has been submitted to considerable editorial treatment, the degree of which we can never know; but as to the choice between tradition or fiction as an ultimate source, we register an emphatic verdict in favor of tradition. This is the longest of the controversial discourses, embracing 7:16-8:58. In 8:59 we have one of those brief historical summaries which could be either editorial or a part of the tradition, and it is vain to speculate which. Of course 7:53-8:11 is an interpolation.

The fourth controversy is introduced by another very distinct narrative pericope. It is typical and complete as contained in 9:1-7. But again we meet with catechemenate expansion. That the story was circulated independently in just the form it presents in 9:1-7 we do not contend, but it is in those verses that it exhibits its typical pericopate elements. The narrative is then extended to include the agitation of the healed man's neighbors. The matter is thus brought to the attention of the Jewish authorities, and the issue is raised, which is again the sabbath question. The discourse takes the form of dialogue and debate.

There is added to the controversy relative to the blind man the beautiful discourse of Jesus on the Good Shepherd (10:1-18). The connection in which we find it here is probably an editorial device of the author. The blindness of the Pharisees (9:40,41) prevents them from discerning the true door to the sheep-fold. The parable proper, which could better be called the "Parable of the One Door", appears in 10:1-5. It is more similar to the Synoptic parables than any other figurative teaching recorded in this Gospel. The general structure of the entire teaching unit is after the manner of primitive Christian teaching, if we are to use the Synoptic form as a criterion. Jesus speaks the parable, having begun perhaps with some such statement as,"The kingdom of heaven is like unto a sheep-fold". Because of the growing misunderstanding and jealousy of the Roman officials the Christians of Asia were avoiding the use of the word "kingdom".[21] This could account for the absence of the familiar parabolic introduction. In 10:6 is a comment which sounds like an echo from Mark, "This proverb ($\pi\alpha\rho o\iota\mu\iota\alpha\nu$) Jesus spoke to them, but they did not understand what it was that he told them". (Cf. Mk. 4:33.) Jesus then explains the parable. The substance of the parable itself and the application may certainly be taken as based on original teaching of Jesus. Verse 6 is the esoteric interpretation applied by Hellenistic Christianity to the caution which Jesus observed in appearing in the role of Messiah, a role so fraught with potential violence in first century Palestine.

In 10:11-18, 27-29 we have, woven together, the original Parable of the Good Shepherd and its explanation. It is not the form of parabolic teaching which we find in the Synoptics, but quite plausibly may be regarded as interwoven fragments of an original parable and its expla-

---

21 Cf. Colwell, John Defends the Gospel, pp. 102-109.

nation, modified and adapted by catechumentate expansion. John has taken this survival of the parables of the One Door and the Good Shepherd and blended them into his record of the Great Controversies. The degree of editorial modification we are without criteria for determining.

This discourse has the brief historical climax characteristic of John's discourse sections.

A very brief pericope of didactic narrative introduces the fifth controversy (10:22-25). It raises the issue of true discipleship, and a controversial discourse follows. The discourse leads on to another declaration of Jesus relative to his identity with the Father, and closes with the brief historical climax.

Though the block of material 5:1-10:39 defies logical analysis, the mechanical literary structure of it is manifest beyond dispute. There are the five controversies, built against the background of the five narrative introductions. The organization of the material is the work of the author, and undoubtedly there are editorial revisions, additions and connections, but in the main the material was derived from tradition current at that period in Ephesian Christianity.

The next block of material is distinctively narrative. It extends from 10:40 to 13:30. When analyzed as to form it presents four types of traditional material. There are three pericopae. Two of them (12:1-8, 12-19) we have already discussed as typical examples of hortatory narrative. In the enquiry of the Greeks we may see a didactic narrative if we contemplate only the passage 12:20-26, and that was probably its original limits. As incorporated here it has been submitted to catechumenate expansion. Two sections in this block of material must be classified as historical narrative. Both are longer, more elaborate, and more formal in continuity than pericopate structure presents. The first (11:1-54) is probably an expanded hortatory narrative. It was doubtless developed into a historical narrative as a sort of prelude to the Passion Narrative. In 13:1-30 we have the other instance of historical narration, which also probably arose and developed in connection with the Passion Narrative. There are four editorial insertions (10:40-42; 11:55-57; 12:9-11; 36b-43). We propose as the best explanation for these brief connecting passages that they were composed by the author out of his own general familiarity with the evangelic tradition. Interwoven into this predominantly narrative material there are two discouse passages (12:27-36a, 44-50) which we simply classify as caetchumenal instruction. We believe such a classification points in the direction of the traditional sources. It has all been welded into a continuous story by the literary art of the author, and without doubt bears many traces of the touch of his editorial hand.

The next great block of material (13:31-17:26) is almost wholly discourse. The narrative touches in it furnish variety and background for the long record of didactic material. As the material appears before us here it is a product of teaching and preaching in the churches of Asia. The author and those associated with him had for a generation or more taught these profound sayings on the claim of the authority of Jesus. The way the material is organized here into the form of a final discourse, a last "Table Talk", is probably entirely due to the author. That the writer on the inspiration of the moment, or even after long and mature reflection, devised out of his own metaphysical cogitations these profound teachings is inconceivable. But do they go back to the teachings of Jesus? They go back to Jesus the Teacher! It would require a supernaturalistic assumption which would be crassly mechanical to maintain that we have here the actual words of Jesus, for, as we have observed above, the stylistic evidence against the position is conclusive. But somehow what Jesus taught the minds of his disciples was blended with what Jesus became in the experience of his disciples, and set in motion tides of spiritual influence which are cresting in these chapters. The Ephesian teachers who propagated the substance of this great last discourse believed themselves to be teaching what Jesus revealed concerning himself and his divine Spirit in the experience of the believer. And they were eminently correct! It were vain and futile to go back behind this discourse material and try to reconstruct actual Aramaic sayings of Jesus upon which any or all of it is based, but the only explanation of these chapters is Jesus, just as surely as though every Greek word had been formed upon his lips. We are not prepared to contend that in any sense he spoke the language contained in these chapters, but we are perfectly certain that he created the teaching recorded here. Without Jesus these teachings could never have been: not a word occurs here that does not rest ultimately on the creative force of his marvelous personality. Jesus did not speak these things directly to the unprepared ears of Galilean disciples, but he spoke them across the years to the cultured heart of the Ephesian church, and a noble leader of that church made record of what they heard.[22]

The final block of material is perfectly distinct in character and limits. It is the Passion Narrative and Resurrection Account of the Fourth Gospel. In form it is simply historical narration, just as we have in the Synoptic Gospels. There are many points of contact with the Synoptics, and the general course of events is the same but there is wide variance in details. That the story as told here was largely manufactured by the author in defiance of the Synoptic record, I am sure no critic would claim. Indeed, it must be remembered that there is no fixed and clearly defined "Synoptic record" here, for the Synoptic Gospels differ widely in the midst of their agreements. We believe we can rest our case here: We have before us in these chapters the record of an Ephesian tradition of the Passion and Resurrection.[23] Especially in chapter 20 we find such a comprehensive, well-formed and coherent Resurrection Account that it could hardly be thought of otherwise than as the Ephesian tradition of the Resurrection. It will certainly not be gravely questioned that there is a traditional basis for this block of material.

22 Cf. Hopwood, **The Religious Experience of the Primitive Church,** pp. 16-21. We find ourselves in intimately close accord with Dr. Hopwood's explanation, except that we would put the experience of the Ephesian Christian community where he puts the experience of the author.

23 C. H. Dodd believes that here the fourth evangelist "has in substance followed an independent tradition". (**History and the Gospels, p. 80.**)

The Appendix (21:1-23) is a typical piece of historical narration. It really seems to have been a sort of personal history narrative which had developed in connection with Peter. The very significant play on words in the reported conversation between Jesus and Peter would strongly suggest that it was originally composed in Greek, and therefore could not have been Palestinian in origin. However, there is a distinction between two Aramaic words for love which would have made that aspect of the conversation possible. At any rate, we may regard it as a piece of historical narration current in Ephesian tradition, which derived its basal substance from an original Galilean tradition. The author himself added it to his Gospel, probably before the Gospel was ever released for circulation.[24] The question of the reasons for adding the Appendix are not within the province of this discussion. The closing postscript (21:24,25) is quite obviously editorial.

24 But per contra see Bacon, Gospel of the Hellenists, pp. 12-15.

~ VII ~

We have come to see in the progress of our investigation that the Fourth Gospel is independent of the Synoptics, yet related to them. The obvious contacts in the midst of so many differences are significant. The hypothesis we are developing here is that the Fourth Gospel is the literary composition of an Ephesian tradition which had roots extending back into the original Palestinian tradition. In the course of its development this Ephesian tradition has been affected by two strong currents of influence. The first emanated from Paul. There was nothing produced in the last forty years of apostolic history which escaped the influence of Paul, and the Fourth Gospel exhibits it clearly. Then there was the influence of the environment of Ephesian Christianity at the time of writing. This environmental influence involved a strong philosophical factor which was deeply affected by Gnosticism, but also was fighting an earnest battle not to be submerged by Gnosticism. Hence the philosophical strain is both Gnostic and anti-Gnostic in its manifestations. There were also doctrinal issues which had produced distinct effects upon Ephesian tradition.

It appears then that we may look for three strata of tradition in the Fourth Gospel. The first is a substratum or original Palestinian tradition, the second is a stratum determined by Pauline influence, and the third an Ephesian stratum, involving the existing issues of Ephesian Christianity at the close of the first century, and manifesting the results of Gnostic reaction — a sort of Christian-

Gnostic stratum. Evidences for these three strata may be positively discerned, though the exact seams which divide them cannot be pointed out, for it is not a mechanically compiled but a blended tradition.

At the basis of the Ephesian tradition we may clearly detect the Palestinian substrtum. We would be inclined to assume from the very nature of the facts of first century Christian life and thought that Palestinian tradition would survive as a substratum in any gospel material. There are considerations which point insistently in this direction: (1) the Palestinian tradition was at the fountain-head of apostolic teaching; (2) it embraced the basal facts upon which the Christian religion was founded; (3) it was always a respected source. Then when we examine the material of John's Gospel we find such a substratum definitely reflected there.

It is now an axiom of Gospel criticism that the material of the Synoptic Gospels was originally a Palestinian tradition. With all its independence and distinctiveness, the Fourth Gospel nevertheless presents several parallels to the Synoptics, especially in the Passion section. But while these are unquestionably parallel in substance, the differences are too great to admit of the theory that John derived them from the Synoptic Gospels.[1] Such a theory must assume that John snatched from the Synoptics, particularly Mark, a few detached parallels, chosen at random, and woven into the course of his Gospel without consider-

1 This position has recently been re-inforced with strong support by P. Gardner-Smith in his book, **St. John and the Synoptic Gospels** (Cambridge, 1938). The entire volume of one hundred and twelve pages is devoted to the proof of this one thesis.

ation of original expression or connection. This simply means that there is no consistent hypothesis for explaining how John took these parallels from the Synoptic Gospels.[2] Certainly there are quite a number of evident contacts between Mark and John, but these can best be explained as a result of interaction between the two basal traditions somewhere near their original source.[3] Divergent development had long ago succeeded interaction. It is far more reasonable to suppose that John's source was neither of the written Gospels, Matthew, Mark nor Luke, but was essentially related to the original source from which their contents were derived. That is, the material in John parallel to the synoptic Gospels was a survival of Palestinian tradition, revised and adapted to Ephesian Christianity of 100 A.D.

Examination of a few of these parallels will disclose the processes of adaption, and at the same time reveal the essential Palestinian character of the tradition. Take for instance the record of John the Baptist.[4] The relation of the ministry of Jesus to that of John the Baptist was an embarrassingly awkward fact to the fourth evangelist. He could happily have left it out, for reasons familiar to any New Testament scholar. When he does introduce it, he is careful to guard against any damaging implications and to adapt it to the needs and purposes of Ephesian

2 An important consideration bearing on this point is contained in the observation of Windisch: "Die Annahme, dass alle oder die meisten synopt. Erzaehlungen . . . in Joh. interpoliert seien und zwar dem Zwecke, den Joh. mehr an die Synopse an zugleichen, schient mir unhaltbar". (Johannes und die Synoptiker: Untersuchungen zum Neuen Testament, vol. xii, p. 56f.)

3 "Any supposed dependence of this Gospel on the Synoptics may be due to the fact that the Synoptic tradition was well known also to the compilers of the Johannine narrative." Hopwood, op. cit., p. 16.

4 Cf. Gardner-Smith, op. cit., pp. 1-11.

Christianity in his time. Why bring it in at all? Through Palestinian tradition it had become fixed in the account of the Messianic career, so that John could not in fairness or safety neglect it. It was already a part of the tradition current in Ephesian Christianity, and therefore was ready to hand for the fourth evangelist, already adapted by traditional processes to the ends he had in view. The writer of the Fourth Gospel was not the first one to discover the need of adapting the history of John the Baptist to the prevailing situation in Ephesian Christianity. This need had long been existing in the Asian churches, and therefore we must suppose that the readjustment of the tradition had already progressed practically to the form which we find in the written Gospel. The fourth evangelist was not remolding tradition, but recording remolded tradition—Palestinian tradition adapted to the apologetic and polemical needs of late first century Ephesian Christianity.

The closest parallel in the Fourth Gospel to the language of the Synoptics is in the account of the Cleansing of the Temple (2:13-18). Yet the results of adaptation are clearly traceable. The record is in substance closely parallel to Mark through verses 13-16. At verse 17 manifest deviation begins. The interest which defines this deviation is manifest and significant. A secret insight was granted to the disciples as they witnessed the event. They "remembered that it had been written, The zeal of thy house shall devour me". The esoteric interest evident here is one of those subtle traces of Gnostic influence which frequently appear in the Fourth Gospel. But it is interesting to note how the Jewish interest in fulfillment of prophecy is blended with it. In the next verse the theophanic interest characteristic of Ephesian tradition appears, when "the Jews demand a sign". The reply is couched in symbolic language which "the Jews" are unable to comprehend, but the full meaning of which was disclosed to the disciples after the Resurrection. In this passage there appears a remarkable interweaving of four distinct lines of interest: esoteric, theophanic, anti-Semitic, and prophetic. Each reflects a separate source of influence: the first is Gnostic, the second is Græco-Roman religious, the third is Greek-Christian, and the fourth is Jewish. This cosmopolitan reflection exhibits in a vivid fashion the processes which wrought the Ephesian tradition.

Particularly is adaptation exhibited in the altered setting of the Cleansing of the Temple. As to the chronological position of the event, we must favor the Synoptic setting, for in their account it fits easily into the natural course of development in the career of Jesus. As employed by John, its chronological relations are overshadowed by doctrinal concern: it is a demonstration of Messianic authority and power which had a vital place in preparing the minds of the disciples for an eventual understanding of Jesus. As a result of this display of supernatural authority they "believed the scripture and the word which Jesus spoke". Thus in doctrinal import it quite appropriately moves into juxtaposition with the Miracle at Cana. It is clearly material which the writer is adapting to the polemical purposes of his own time. Its Palestinian origin is beyond question, and its Ephesian adaptation is vividly manifest.[4]

The Triumphal Entry would not be naturally an incident of any great interest to Ephesian Christianity at the end of the first century. The whole interest of the story is essentially Jewish and belongs to Palestinian Judaism. It is motivated and pervaded by intense Jewish Messianism, which would claim little concern in Ephesian Christian circles at the time of the Fourth Gospel. The Ephesian Christian who wrote the Gospel would not have included the Triumphal Entry because of any individual or group interest. It was a heritage from Palestinian tradition, and served the author beautifully as an additional proof of the futility of the opposition to Jesus.

The term "Son of man", used thirteen times in the Gospel,[5] is definitely Palestinian in its significance and interest. It is a Messianic title, belonging to literary rather than to popular Judaism. It was probably to some extent obscure even to Jesus' own contemporaries.[6] To Ephesian Christianity at 100 A.D. it was only a traditional title of the Master. Its original Messianic significance was unknown and indifferent as far as they were concerned. It is doubtful whether even the writer had any interest in the expression as a title of the Messiah. To his age even the term Christ was a sacred name rather than a Messianic title. It is highly significant that the phrase "Son of man"

4 Cf. Gardner-Smith, op cit., pp. 12-16.

5 Jn. 1:51; 3:13, 14; 5:27; 6:27, 53, 62; 8:28; 9:35; 12:23, 34 (dis); 13:31.

6 The Messianic significance of the term "Son of Man" would be obscure to Ephesian Christianity, but a kindred idea undoubtedly existed in the religious metaphysics of the Hellenistic Orient of John's time. Cf. Kraeling, Anthropos and Son of Man, pp. 167-174. But note Kraeling's observation that "the Johannine use of Son of Man is rooted in the Synoptic tradition" (p. 167).

occurs only in the reported words of Jesus. It must be explained then as an element of the Palestinian heritage in the Ephesian tradition, a survival of the original and authentic tradition of the teaching of Jesus. No other explanation is tenable.

It is a strikingly significant fact that John is the one Gospel which reflects most vividly Jewish Messianism of first century Palestine. The Messianic conceptions of Palestinian Judaism are in the background of nearly every chapter of the book. In the account of the delegation of Jewish authorities sent to interview John the Baptist (1:19-28) there appear intensely Messianic touches. The concern of the Jerusalem officials about the possibility of Messianic claims, the suggestion of the alternative "Elijah" role which John might be seeking to pursue, the possibility of his claiming to be "the Prophet" promised by Moses (Deut. 18:15), and John's own claim to the pre-Messianic function prophesied by Isaiah (40:3), all belong distinctively to Jewish Messianism, presenting issues of universal interest in Palestine at 25-30 A.D., but only vaguely comprehended in Ephesian Christian circles at 100 A. D.

Philip's announcement to Nathanael and Nathanael's response (1:45f.) portray very characteristic reactions for Palestinian Judaism of Jesus' time, but matters of no imaginable interest to Ephesian Christianity of John's time. The Samaritan participation in the Messianic Hope of Judaism, reflected in 4:25, was a paradox quite familiar to Palestinian Christianity, but which would hardly have occurred in such life-like vividness to the fancy of an

Ephesian Christian at the close of the first century. The assumed Mosaic basis of the Messianic Hope (5:45,46) was deeply fixed in Palestinian Jewish thought, but had no conceivable basis of interest in Ephesian Christian thought. The natural enthusiasm of a throng of poorly nourished Galilean Jews in the effort to claim a Messianic king who could feed them by supernatural processes (6:15) fits into the known facts of first century Palestinian life so well that it is hardly a convincing hypothesis to explain it as a product of the fancy of an Ephesian Christian seventy-five years after the crucifixion. The popular notion that the Messiah would be attested by spectacular and mystifying proofs (7:26, 27, 31) is an intensely typical element of the Messianic view of Palestinian Judaism. Aversion to the thought of a Messiah of Galilean origin (7:40-42) reflects a very natural reaction of Messianic thought in Judea, especially Jerusalem. We have already noted how intensely Messianic in interest and reflections is the account of the Triumphal Entry (12:12ff.). The conception of a permanent earthly reign of the Messiah (12:34) was an aspect of Jewish Messianic thought which could have had no place in the Ephesian Christian mind in the background of the Fourth Gospel. The Johannine viewpoint is but little influenced by even the doctrine of the second advent of Christ so could certainly have had no interest in a permanent Jewish Messiah on earth. Such an element as this points unerringly to Palestine.

These are but a few examples of the abundance of Messianic reflections in the Gospel of John. Exhaustive treatment would require an entire volume of normal size.

It is not possible to conceive of Ephesian Christianity as having been so imbued with distinctively Jewish Messianism, though the author of the Gospel possessed enough Messianic interest (20:31) to constitute him a secure custodian of such a tradition.

We have noted in general the Palestinian element of the Ephesian tradition attested in the definite parallels to the Synoptic Gospels, the use of the term "Son of man", and the pervading Messianic reflections in the Fourth Gospel. This Palestinian substratum is even more impressively exhibited in certain specific passages of the Gospel. The Johannine account of John the Baptist presents one trait more primitive than the Matthean account. While Matthew's tradition contemplates John as hesitating to baptise Jesus in full knowledge that he is the Messiah, the tradition imbedded in the Johannine account pictures John as having preached in the prophetic consciousness that the Messianic advent was at hand, but as not realizing that Jesus was the fulfillment of his message until after he had baptised Jesus. There is strong reason for regarding the Johannine representation as nearest the actual experience of the Baptist. John most likely preached in an eager anticipation of a Messianic advent far more spectacular and revolutionary than the quiet approach of the Messiah to him to request baptism at his hands. Whatever conviction he had of Jesus as the Messiah must have come subsequent to the Master's baptism. Hence the Johannine tradition seems to lie closest to the original facts in the consciousness of John the Baptist, and is entirely alien to any experience conceivable in Ephesian Christianity seventy-five years later.

The pronounced Judaistic coloring of 1:51 is quite obvious. "Ye shall see the heaven opened, and the angels of God ascending and descending upon the Son of man." There are here two distinctly Palestinian traits. (1) The passage is quite definitely apocalyptic in the form of conception. The Fourth Gospel as a whole is practically devoid of apocalyptic interest and mode of expression. This form of religious thought was indigenous to Palestinian Judaism. Even the Synoptic Gospels do not contain a great deal of apocalyptic material. It never appealed to Gentile Christianity. The best way to account for its presence here in the Fourth Gospel is that it is a survival of typical Palestinian tradition, employed by the Ephesian author, not from apocalyptic interest, but because of its emphasis upon the transcendence of the One whom he worshipped as the incarnate and exalted Logos of God. (2) As we have already noted, the phrase "Son of man" is inseparably associated with Palestinian Messianism, and indubitably reflects the influence of a distinctive Jewish source.

We find in 3:25 another passage with a srtong Jewish coloring. "There arose therefore a questioning on the part of John's disciples with a Jew about purifying." John was performing a ceremonial ablution which only an ordained priest or rabbi was supposed to perform. This would raise an acute question in Judea; it would be of no interest whatever in Ephesus. Doubtless Ephesian Christianity in the time of the fourth evangelist but vaguely understood. the passage. It was a brief item of tradition brought to Ephesus from Palestine.

Jesus' assertion to the woman of Sychar, "Ye worship
ye know not what" (4:22), reflects a remarkably typical
Jewish prejudice which had a factual basis in the character
and history of the Samaritans. In fact, the entire story
of the Samaritan woman is vivid with Palestinian traits.
It fits with obvious plausibility into the hypothesis of a
Judean tradition with an Ephesian veneer.

At 4:44 is a passage which has always given trouble
to commentators. It is entirely out of connection with
its context. The writer has been recording the Samaritan
ministry of Jesus, and has just described his departure
from Samaria into Galilee. Then he adds, "For Jesus
himself testified, that a prophet hath no honor in his own
country". Does the writer consider Samaria as Jesus' own
country? This is inconceivable and out of accord with the
larger context (1:45,46; 18:5,7; 19:19). Yet as one reads
the verse in its present connection such seems to be the
import. Yet we know the writer could not have meant it
this way, but was intending to give the reason for Jesus
entering Galilee from Judea. At this point another difficulty arises. The saying in its Synoptic setting applies
to the rejection at Nazareth, which the fourth evangelist
agrees in representing as the original home of Jesus.
Here it seems to refer to Judea as Jesus' homeland. How
account for the apparent inconsistency and the shift in
application? If we compare Luke's account we will find
that just at this point (of the departure of Jesus from
Judea into Galilee) occurs the rejection at Nazareth. In
the original Palestinian tradition this saying was an explanation of his treatment at the hands of his former
Nazareth neighbors. In the Ephesian tradition it was the

only remaining trace left of the rejection at Nazareth, and fell into a place very satisfactory to the interests of the Johannine tradition as an explanation of the departure from Judea, reflecting an intimation that Judea had become the adopted homeland of Jesus. It is a strand of Palestinian tradition woven into the Ephesian tradition with an altered import.[7]

The reference in 9:22 to the rigorous caution of the Jewish authorities in suppressing Messianic agitation is very realistic to one familiar with conditions in Palestine during the time of Christ. Tragic consequences had more than once resulted from abortive Messianic movements, so that the Jewish leaders had come to recognize in any sort of Messianic agitation a grave menace to the security of the nation. Hence the least appearance of it must be summarily suppressed and severely punished. To a Palestinian Jew to be "put out of the synagogue" was a dreaded penalty. It meant both religious privation and social ostracism. Hence the alarm of the healed man's parents was quite obvious to the Jews of Palestine. To Christians in Ephesus the reference would be but dimly comprehended. Such phraseology and *Sitz im Leben* could only by strained explanation be accounted for as a product of Ephesian thought in John's day. It is most reasonable to see in it a surviving trace of Palestinian tradition.

Quite a similar instance appears in 16:2. "They shall put you out of the synagogues: yea, the hour cometh that whosoever killeth you shall think that he offereth service unto God." We are unable to picture a natural

7 Gardner-Smith, op. cit., pp. 20-22.

setting for this passage in Ephesian Christianity at 100 A.D. Expelling Christians from synagogues and executing them as traitors to Judaism scarcely fits into pagan Gentile surroundings. It had been a long, long while since Asian disciples had been put out of synagogues, and it is doubtful that they had ever been killed by Jewish persecutors. There could not be imagined any local interest in this prediction in Ephesian Christianity of John's day, but it finds a vivid background in the conditions that are generally considered to have prevailed in Palestine during the early days of apostolic history.

Again we find reasonable limits of space preventing an exhaustive treatment of evidences, but these instances point in a very definite direction. They strongly suggest a Palestinian source for the basal stratum of the Ephesian tradition contained in the Fourth Gospel.

To this review of direct evidence of a Palestinian substratum of the Ephesian tradition we may add a strong array of indirect evidence. In Dean Colwell's brief treatise, *John Defends the Gospel,* he has made out a very convincing case relative to the purpose and influences which governed the fourth evangelist. In view of his conclusions, there is impressive significance attaching to certain traits of the Gospel which are manifestly out of harmony with the dominant interests of the author. Examination of these extraneous elements points definitely to Palestinian Christianity as their origin.

John's Gospel is clearly influenced by the menace of imperial jealousy. Any indication of royal aspiration anywhere in the Roman empire was dealt with summarily by the relentless hand of Rome. Hence when John wrote there must be exceeding caution in applying to the Christian movement the term "kingdom". It is of far less frequent occurrence in the Fourth Gospel than in the Synoptic Gospels. Yet in Jesus' conversation with Nicodemus the term appears twice in one paragraph (3:3,5). Colwell recognizes that in the use of it here, "John is editing an earlier saying".[8] At 6:15 there is the acknowledgement of implications that during his lifetime Jesus had been connected with the Jewish conception of a Messianic king, and that an effort had been made by his followers to precipitate him into the active performance of such a role. This could easily have provoked the suspicion that monarchial aspirations might still be latent in the Christian movement. The passage itself, as we have before observed, is intensely Palestinian in flavor, but to a Roman of Ephesus this fact would be utterly unknown; but the association of kingly prerogatives with Jesus could attract very unfavorable attention. No conceivable motive indigenous in his Ephesian environment could have prompted John to invent such a form of presentation. It must be accounted for as a surviving element of original Palestinian tradition.

Nothing is more distinctive in the Fourth Gospel than its aversion to Palestinian Judaism. This arose from two causes: the antagonism of standard Judaism toward Jesus and his religion, and a subconscious adaptation to the extreme anti-Semitism of the surrounding Gentile world. Consequently, in John's Gospel Jesus and his followers are

8 Op. cit., p. 136.

regularly set off in contradistinction to "the Jews".[9] There is a tendency throughout the book to avoid any identification with Judaism, which distinguishes John in a marked way from the Synoptics. Yet Jewish traits and distinctive Jewish interests abound throughout the Fourth Gospel, as we have elsewhere shown. It has been observed above that the Messianic Hope of Judaism, especially in its popular aspects, is more vividly reflected in John than in the Synoptics. Nine times in the Gospel Jesus is addressed as "Rabbi",[10] a distinctly and exclusively Jewish title of respect for a teacher. Only Matthew and Mark of the Synoptists used it, and they only nine times — Matthew four times and Mark five times.[11] Jewish background and Jewish coloring are manifest throughout the Gospel. The anxiety of the Jerusalem authorities over the ministry of John the Baptist (1:19ff.), the conception of Jesus as a sacrifice on the altar of atonement (1:29,36) and as the Messiah promised in the scriptures (1:45), and the apocalyptic representation of his triumph in a figure from the Jewish scriptures, are illustrative instances which show how much Jewish influence can be found in but one chapter. Every succeeding chapter would yield comparable results. It would require a volume of large proportions to treat the matter adequately. These distinct Jewish traces are not due to the interest of the author; they are inseparable elements of his traditional heritage.

John is conspicuously the Gospel of the divine Christ, the pre-existent Son of God. To the author his Master

9 Colwell, op. cit., pp. 45ff.

10 Jn. 1:38, 49; 3:2, 26; 4:31; 6:25; 9:2; 11:8; 20:16 (long form).

11 This could be accounted for by the fact that the term was but little used when Synoptic tradition arose.

was a transcendent Lord—a celestial being occupying a
human body and moving among the scenes of earth (cf.
1:14). Yet vivid traces of humanity abound in the Johannine description of Jesus. Almost as soon as he is introduced we find him connected with an ordinary earthly
dwelling place (1:39). One of his most transcendent
achievements involved his attendance as an invited guest
at a wedding-feast (2:1ff.), and occasioned reference to
his human mother (2:3). Just a little later he is found
in intimate association with his human mother and brothers
(2:12). The revelation of his Messianic glory and prerogative to Samaria was occasioned by an incident in
which he is represented as tired and hungry (4:6,8).
Nowhere in John's Gospel does Jesus more emphatically
claim for himself transcendent character than in his discourse on the Bread of Life, in the very midst of which
we find reference to a human father and mother (6:42).
In 6:67 the pathetic question of Jesus to the Twelve,
"You are not wanting to go away too, are you?" reflects
a surge of disappointment in the heart of the Master
which is quite typically human. This was doubtless an
unwitting implication as far as the author was concerned,
but it nevertheless reflects a human reaction. In 7:2-10
there is implied a change of mind on the part of Jesus
which a Christian scribe in copying the Fourth Gospel
sought to eliminate by an emendation of the text, and
which has baffled ardent apologists down to the present
day. In a preface to one of his most profound discourses
concerning his own transcendent nature and functions,
Jesus is represented as receiving information and search-
ing for one he has healed (9:35). In connection with his

most marvelous miracle, Jesus adapts his plans to news which is conveyed to him by human informants (11:3,6, 17). For a brief period at the close of his ministry, he retires to solitude in an effort to escape the wrath of his enemies (11:54). Andrew and Philip inform their Master of the approach of the enquiring Greeks, and Jesus reacts in joyful surprise at the information (12:20ff.). Such traces of human experience and reaction could be greatly multiplied by an exhaustive treatment of this aspect of the Gospel, but these are enough to show that the Redeemer-God of the Fourth Gospel is at the same time an incarnate God—the God-man of Synoptic tradition, with emphasis on the first member of the hyphen. The emphasis on divinity is due to the interests and requirements belonging to the writer's environment; the presence of the human is a survival of original Palestinian tradition.

Thus direct and indirect evidences point to a Palestinian substratum in the traditional basis of the Fourth Gospel.

The influence of Paul on the Gospel of John is an axiom of New Testament criticism. It is not without its problems and possibilities of a variety of opinions, but the fact is disputed by no one. The detailed evidences are so familiar that they need but bare mention. They fall naturally into two classifications.

(1) In a few instances the influence of Paul upon John is disclosed in detailed parallels of thought and phraseology. This may be seen by a comparison of the following passages: Jn. 6:29 with Eph. 2:8; II Thes. 1:11; or Jn. 8:33-39 with Rom. 6:16-23; Gal. 4:30; 5:1; or Jn. 8:56

with Rom. 4:20; or Jn. 10:12,13 with Ac. 20:28,29. The
echoes of Pauline modes of expression found here could
only by a very strained supposition be accounted for by
any personal influence of Paul over the author of the
Fourth Gospel; they may far more probably be explained
as arising from a tradition in which Pauline phraseology
and thought had become interwoven as a result of the
Apostle's long contact with Ephesus.

(2) The chief substance of the Pauline stratum in the
Fourth Gospel consists of certain great doctrinal conceptions and viewpoints. The pre-existence and transcendence of Christ is subject to an emphasis in John which we
do not find in the Synoptics, but which is only a slightly
advanced development of Paul's teaching on these points.
In John's presentation of the Person of Christ we have a
Pauline conception overlaid with an Ephesian veneer, the
Ephesian element appearing in the more metaphysical
aspects of the teaching. The revolutionary spiritual
change wrought by the believer's relation to Christ, described in John as a new birth (3:3-8), is parallel to the
experience described by Paul as a new creation in Christ
Jesus (2 Co. 5:17). Indeed, it is just here that Paul made
one of his most important advances beyond the earliest
apostolic tradition. It was in some primitive non-pneu-
matic tradition that Apollos had been instructed when
he came to Ephesus "knowing only the baptism of John"
(Ac. 18:25). It was the Pauline doctrine of spiritual
transformation and induement—the work of the Holy
Spirit—which Aquila and Priscilla imparted to Apollos
when they "expounded unto him the way of God more
accurately" (Ac. 18:26). The influence of this Pauline

doctrine in Ephesus, with a Hellenistic adaptation which we are to discuss in the sequel, set the mold for the teaching presented in Jn. 3:3-8.

Paul and John agree in regarding participation in the kingdom and redemptive benefits of Christ as conditioned upon faith. While the noun faith ($\pi i \sigma \tau i s$) does not occur in John, the verb abounds, being used some ninety times. It is also true that the mode of conception differs in Paul and John, Paul conceiving of the experience in a juridical form as justification by faith, while John sees it as believing unto eternal life. But basally it is a common doctrine to both Paul and John.

Paul and John agree in seeing the death of Christ as a voluntary offering of himself in atonement for sin. Probably this is the point at which the Pauline influence is most forceful and distinctive in the Fourth Gospel. Jesus is introduced by John the Baptist as the sacrificial lamb, offered for sin (Jn. 1:29,36); the temple of his body is to be destroyed and restored (2:19); he is to be lifted up like the brazen serpent in the wilderness (3:14), such lifting up on the cross being indispensably necessary to his ultimate triumph (12:32,33). Throughout the Gospel Christ is seen as a voluntary offering for sin.

These examples suggest the actuality and extent of the Pauline stratum in the Fourth Gospel.[12]

12 Further statement of the case may be found in Scott, The Fourth Gospel: Its Purpose and Theology, pp. 46-53, and Bacon in the Anglican Theol. Review, vol. xi, pp. 199-223, 305-320. Scott's treatment is brief and general while Bacon deals with some special aspects of the question.

There is presented in the Fourth Gospel a third distinctive stratum of tradition, which composes what we may call the surface stratum, and is the largest element in it—the element which distinguishes its character. This we shall call the Ephesian stratum. It is distinguished by two characteristics. It is philosophical in its general character, and it reflects the conflicting currents of thought which were agitating Ephesian Christianity at the close of the first century.

Doubtless the feature which differentiates the Fourth Gospel most sharply from the Synoptics is its presentation of the Person of Christ. We have not only the culmination of a long process of development, but a different mode of viewing the matter. Christ is not merely the Messiah of Israel, who revealed his purpose to become by missionary propagation the redeemer of mankind, but he is the incarnate Son of God who was never received by Israel, but became in spite of that fact the Revealer of God to men. Jesus the Galilean teacher is all but eclipsed by Christ the Redeemer-God, the pre-existent Logos.[13]

This is not the independent philosophical speculation of some Ephesian Christian around A.D. 100, but the conception developed in the churches of Asia through the last half of the first century, defined and promoted by Pauline and Hellenistic influence. Paul undoubtedly found these developments in progress, and sought to combat that which he opposed and direct that which he considered to be in harmony with the true gospel. Colos-

13 The Hellenistic Christology of Paul and John as to both its distinctive character and sources, is ably discussed by Bacon, Gospel of the Hellenists, pp. 101-110.

sians and Ephesians represent Paul's effort to adapt himself to and aid in the progress of these developments. The "un-Pauline" elements of these two epistles are not the pseudonymous production of a late first century Ephesian Christian, but the adaptation of elements in Ephesian Christian thought by the hand of Paul himself. He spent a longer period of time in Ephesus than in any other one locality where he labored as an apostle, and had ample opportunity to have received into his own thinking elements from the thought life of Ephesian Christianity. If we mark the development of his Christological thought through I Co. 8:6, 2 Co. 1-9, Philippians, Colossians, and Ephesians, we can trace the growing effects of those Ephesian influences. Ephesian Christianity was teaching Paul while Paul was teaching Ephesian Christianity. Indeed twentieth century New Testament scholarship has established at least the possibility that the Prison Epistles were written in Ephesus rather than Rome. Whoever wrote them and wherever they were written, the fact is beyond dispute that they reflect Ephesian Christian thought prior to the time of John's Gospel. It is clearly the type of thought which determined the surface stratum of the Ephesian tradition.

We may therefore conclude that the Logos doctrine was not something which an Ephesian elder sat down and thought out and committed to writing like a modern essay. The presentation of it in the Fourth Gospel is a condensed record of a conception which was familiar throughout the churches of Asia in the last decade of the first century. It was one of the largest products of the development of Ephesian Christian thought, and a product

which was Gnostic-Christian in character. Bacon has
shown us that even this element may have its relation to
Palestine, but if so the relation belongs to external historical developments, for essentially the idea is distinctly
germane to Greek thought. It is Christian teaching in a
Hellenistic mold.

John's Gospel it not only distinctive in its mode of
presenting the Person of Christ, but in its emphasis upon
that subject. The Gospel is considerably more than fifty
per cent. discourse material. The prevailing theme of this
discourse material is the Person of Christ. We have observed above that there are two great discourse sections
in the book. One is in chapters 5-10 and the other in
chapters 14-17. In the first Jesus is in controversy with
the Jews as to his true divine and redemptive significance,
a significance which they eventually reject and bitterly
oppose. The futility of their opposition is shown in
chapters 11 and 12. The other discourse is devoted to the
inner circle, in which is present "the disciple whom Jesus
loved." The interest here is their preservation and preparation to disseminate the redemptive revelation out beyond
the confines of Israel, who will continue to oppose and
reject. One with even a slight amount of historical
imagination can perceive how such a body of teaching
could be formulated and propagated by the Asian churches
between A.D. 50 and 100. We do not need to overtax
our credulity by supposing that some phenomenal religious
genius out of his own thinking contrived and wrote those
marvelous messages at one sitting. He and other leaders
like him wrought them out in their ministry to and in co-

operation with the Asian churches across the span of at least a generation.

It may be cited now as a fact sufficiently proven that a degenerated survival of John the Baptist's movement existed in the province of Asia at the close of the first century. Because of some claims and representations of these Johannites, the churches of Asia had gradually modified the John the Baptist tradition to safeguard it against these false implications. Such an adapted tradition is clearly in the background of John's Gospel. Even a cursory examination of the account of John the Baptist as recorded by the fourth evangelist discloses a studied caution to avoid any intimation that the Forerunner was the true founder of the Christian religion. The writer again and again buttresses his contention that John the Baptist was but the advance agent of the true redemptive revelation in Jesus. This of course was a concern possessed by all the orthodox churches of Asia, and therefore would undoubtedly characterize the teaching in those churches. Certainly no student of the Gospel would claim that the Ephesian evangelist's was the only voice lifted in propagation of the Christian message at the end of the first century. There was teaching going on throughout the churches, and the author of the Fourth Gospel, the "Elder" *par excellence* of Ephesian Christianity (2 Jn. 1, 3 Jn. 1) was sharing in and greatly influencing that teaching, which was formulated and directed with a view to meeting the requirements of the existing situation. "The agreements between John and the defenders of the faith" certainly must have been "numerous and striking",[14]

14 Colwell, John Defends the Gospel, p. 127.

but the conclusion impresses itself focibly upon us that these agreements were not wholly subsequent to the writing of the Gospel, but in large measure arose from the fact that the defence of the faith which was offered in John's Gospel was already a common tradition used by John and the other defenders of the gospel for a generation before the evangelist wrote. The material of the Fourth Gospel is not a creation but a heritage.

Nothing strikes the average New Testament student with more bewildering surprise than to call on him for an investigation of the doctrine of regeneration in the Synoptic Gospels. Almost invariably he returns to the teacher with the reluctant admission that he has been unable to find any distinct teaching on regeneration in the Synoptics. The reason is quite simple: it is not there. The conception of spiritual transformation is reflected in a few passages, but Synoptic tradition knew no distinct doctrine of the new birth. This was distinctively a Hellenistic conception. We have noted above the possibility of the idea having roots in the authentic teaching of Jesus, and its similarity to the teaching of Paul, but the mode of thought as presented in the Fourth Gospel belonged to the Græco-Roman religious world. It is a distinct example of the elements which comprised the Ephesian stratum.

The famous *Formeschichte* method of dealing with the Synoptic Gospels is based upon a principle which we have no reason for regarding as peculiar to the Synoptic tradition. It was fundamental in first century Christian life. The *Formgeschichte* scholars have called our attention to the quite obvious fact that what we have in Matthew, Mark, and Luke is but a written record of tradition which was being used for teaching and exhortation in the Palestinian churches of early apostolic times.[15] The same picture is before us in the Fourth Gospel. There are other and different factors affecting the development, but the method is essentially the same. The Fourth Gospel is the composition into a product of masterful literary art of materials taught and preached in Asian churches in the last quarter of the first century. In the light of the evidences we have reviewed it appears highly probable that these materials are at once Ephesian, Pauline, and Palestinian. The surface stratum is Ephesian, composed of the latest development of the evangelic material, and distinguished by the interests and problems of late first century Ephesian Christianity; an intermediate stratum may be termed Pauline, because the influence of Paul's teaching is sufficiently manifest to justify linking the source intimately with his name; at the basis of this traditional source lies a Palestinian substratum, distinguished by elements and interests which cannot reasonably be assigned to any aspect of apostolic Christianity outside Palestine. It is upon this Palestinian substratum that we are now to focus our attention.

15 This seems to have been first detected through similarity in Form of the Old Testament stories, especially those in Genesis, as compared with the narratives recorded in our Gospels. Wellhausen shortly after the dawn of the present century, and Gunkel somewhat later, called attention to this phenomenon. Cf. Schmidt, "Die Stellung der Evangelien in der allgemeinen Literaturgeschichte", in Gunkel Eucharisterion, part ii, pp. 86-88.

— VIII —

The progress of our investigation brings us now to the question, How could the influence of Palestinian tradition have so directly affected Ephesian Christianity? The explanation we propose is predicated upon one basal fact. Close study of Ac. 18:19-21 reveals that Christianity in some form had already been planted in Ephesus before Paul went there. "Then they came to Ephesus, and he left them (Aquila and Pricilla) there, after he, having entered into the synagogue, had discoursed with the Jews. Even though they persistently requested him to remain with them a longer time, he consented not, but leaving them with the promise, 'I will return to you again, God willing,' he set out from Ephesus." Certain significant phenomena appear here. Paul teaches unmolested in the synagogue. He receives an intensely sympathetic hearing. Some of his hearers earnestly desire a continuation of his teaching. The situation we deduce from this condensed and somewhat ambiguous notice presents a group of Ephesian Jews already disciples of the Christian movement, but still affiliated with the synagogue. The non-Christian Jews had not yet become aroused to any active opposition against them (cf. Ac. 19:8,9). They were even allowed to offer their Messianic message in the synagogue services. Therefore Paul could present his gospel to the assembled Jewish audience without protest. His manner and message were so convincing that the Christian Jews requested a continuation of his ministry there, but he declined their invitation for the time being, with the promise to accept it at a later date. Such seems to be the picture reflected in Luke's very condensed description, and it indicates the presence of a Christian constituency in the Ephesian Jewish community. We may well suppose that there were also in the Christian group Gentile proselytes and "God-fearers". Their interest in Paul's message strongly implies a concern for Christian teaching, and therefore the existence of a teaching tradition among them.

The record of the ministry of Apollos (Ac. 18:24-26) is strongly corroborative at this point. We have observed above that Luke regarded him as a true Christian disciple, but trained in an inaccurate, or at least an inadequate tradition. Apollos of course had an audience for his teaching, and this audience was undoubtedly composed of more than Aquila and Priscilla. Upon careful contemplation we find some highly significant reflections in this passage. Only a slight use of historical imagination discloses a picture of Apollos with a group of Christian disciples around him, engaged in the study and propagation of an evangelic tradition. This tradition was not in accord with the Pauline gospel at some points, but it was nevertheless a Christian tradition. The inescapable implication of such a picture is that Christian disciples were in Ephesus for a considerable time before Paul began his ministry there, and that they possessed a tradition. Luke would not have regarded such a tradition as being in essential harmony with the "way of the Lord" (Ac. 18:25) had it not exhibited an authentic basis in the original Palestinian tradition. Hence the evidence is strong that there was in Ephesus from the beginning a rather distinctive tradition, with a Palestinian basis. This distinctive tradition persisted and developed until it found permanent form in the Fourth Gospel.

In studying Acts the careful student will remember that the book was written very largely to trace the progress of Christianity from Jerusalem to Rome (Ac. 1:8), following only certain selected lines of development. It is based chiefly upon the account of the missionary achievements of Paul by one of his companions and ardent admirers. The book is not to be taken as a disinterested and comprehensive historical account of the planting of Christianity in the Gentile world. The religion of Jesus already had a wide dissemination in the Gentile world before Paul ever set out. It had preceded him to Damascus, Antioch, Ephesus, Troas, Corinth, Crete and Rome.[1] It originated without his personal contact at Colosse, and probably also at Hierapolis and Laodicea. There is no trace of evidence that he had the remotest part in its introduction into Alexandria. Paul was the greatest of the apostles to the Gentiles, but by no means the only one. Andronicus and Junia were sufficiently effective in missionary activity to be "of note among the apostles", and they were in Christ before Paul (Rom. 16:7), and quite likely were Ephesian Christians. Aquila and Priscilla were Christian missionaries of note and ability, and were already disciples when Paul met them (Ac. 18:2,26). Apollos was converted to Christianity independent of Paul, and taught a tradition different from Paul in his early ministry, and from both Luke and Paul we gain the impression that he was a missionary of zeal and power (Ac. 18:24-28; I Co. 1:12; 3:5,6, etc.).

1 Riddle, **The Gospels**, p. 61.

Our conclusion must be that disciples of Jesus and John the Baptist reached Ephesus prior to Paul's missionary activity there. Conflict and reaction went on for a long time between the two groups. Paul clearly met opposition from the Johannite sect, and we believe it is to become increasingly clear to New Testament scholarship that the Christian tradition first planted in Ephesus differed at many points from the tradition represented by Paul and the Synoptics.

We see therefore that it may certainly be established without reasonable doubt that Palestinian Christianity touched Ephesus independent of and prior to the three years ministry of Paul. Logically consequent upon this fact another fact may reasonably be established. These Palestinian apostles of the cross brought their tradition with them, and preserved and expanded it. We find reflected in the Fourth Gospel a survival of that tradition. This conclusion was reached independent of, but in obvious harmony with the opinion of Bacon expressed in the words, "It [the Fourth Gospel] owed its origin and its peculiar character to the movement begun by the Hellenists of Jerusalem".[2]

We have already observed abundant evidence in the Fourth Gospel itself of this Palestinian element in the Ephesian tradition.[3] These proofs may be yet further developed. Conservative criticism has been able to make out a strong case for the traditional authorship of the Fourth Gospel, and one of its most effective arguments

2 Gospel of the Hellenists, p. 118.

3 Cf. Albright, "Some Observations Favoring the Palestinian Origin of the Fourth Gospel," Harvard Theological Review, xvii (1924), pp. 189-195.

has been based upon the evidence that the author was a Palestinian Jew. Attention has been called to evidences of eye-witness testimony in the Gospel. Opponents of the traditional view have emphatically disputed this supposed eye-witness evidence, and offered plausible explanations to account for it otherwise, but the force of the contention has never been entirely overcome. Many cautious and competent critics still believe that they can detect in the book the traces of the eye-witness. There are tacit evidences, reflections of an eyewitness unconsciously woven into the narrative, such as, "there was much grass in the place" (6:10); then there are patent evidences, where first hand acquaintance with the facts described is either expressly claimed or manifestly implied, as in 19:35. These phenomena have been reviewed in much detail by acknowledged scholars.

Such traces of eye-witness testimony suggests that the writer was a Palestinian Jew and a personal follower of Jesus. But the linguistic evidence is that the writer was decidedly a Hellenistic Jew.[4] The most typical Koine' Greek of the New Testament is that of the Fourth Gospel. So internal evidence seems to point in opposite directions, traces of the eye-witness pointing toward the conclusion that the writer was a Pelestinian Jew, and the language of the book tending to prove that he was a Hellenistic Jew. This apparent contradiction in evidence is accounted for when we recognize that the intensely Greek character of the language is due to the author and his Ephesian circle, while the local reflections are survivals of the original Palestinian tradition.

4 The strongest statement of this case which has yet been made is Colwell, The Greek of the Fourth Gospel.

Of late there has been raging severe conflict in scholarly circles as to whether the Fourth Gospel is Greek or Aramaic in its original language. Strong defenders have appeared on both sides of the question. Among contenders for an Aramaic original are such eminent Semitic scholars as Burney, Torrey, Schlatter, and Abrahams, while on the Greek side of the controversy we find Colwell, Scott, Macgregor, *et alii*.[5] It is true, as Colwell has abundantly demonstrated, that the Greek of the Fourth Gospel is characteristically Koine', but before forming a hasty conclusion on this matter two qualifications must be observed.

(1) There are in the Fourth Gospel some undeniable traces of Semitic idiom. Both Colwell and Scott admit the presence of such traces.[6] In some instances Colwell regards the evidence of Semitic influence as quite probable, though in the main he thinks it very slight. Scott is more generous in his admission of Aramaic traces. However, we are to bear in mind that Dean Colwell undertook his project with the frank purpose of seeing how far he could explain as Koine' Greek idiom the supposed Semitisms in the language of John. Therefore his admissions though few are of more than ordinary significance. His review of the case certainly demonstrates that the original language of the Fourth Gospel was not necessarily Aramaic, but Dean Colwell himself would not claim to have proven that the Greek of John's Gospel cannot be said to reflect a Semitic background. The traces of

---

5 Filson, **op. cit.**, p. 116.

6 Colwell, **op. cit.**, pp. 14, 23, 74, 84; Scott, **Validity of the Gospel Record**, pp. 59, 105, 114, 138.

Semitic idiom could be accounted for by Septuagint influence, but not necessarily so.

(2) The arguments of Torrey, Burney, *et alii,* prove at least that much of the language of the Fourth Gospel *could have been* affected by Aramaic origins. The weight of scholarly opinion in favor of the position that Semitic influence is evident in the language of John is too great to admit of a categorical denial. When such well equipped Semitic scholars as Burney, Torrey, Montgomery and Burrows, supported by others worthy of consideration, claim to find manifest traces of Aramaic idiom, we must conclude that to some extent the Fourth Gospel does exhibit the reflections of Aramaic origin. The weight of scholarly opinion has been sufficient to convince Bacon that is has an "undeniable Semitic coloration".[7] An efective basis of reconciliation is found for this conflict of scholarly opinion if we regard the Fourth Gospel as Aramaic tradition transplanted into Ephesian soil and recorded by a Hellenistic writer.

Scholars of repute have urged an origin of the Gospel in Syria or Palestine because the "Semitic tone" of the book seems to demand a Semitic background for its composition.[8] However, the vast preponderance of critical opinion still holds to Ephesus as the place of composition. Then if the book originated in Ephesus, and is intensely Hellenistic in language and viewpoint, yet exhibits traces of Semitic idiom and a decided Semitic tone, the way is wide open for the explanation of an original Aramaic

7 Gospel of the Hellenists, p. 215.
8 Grant, Growth of the Gospels, pp. 212ff.

tradition, remolded and transcribed in an Ephesian environment. If it is true that "no Palestinian Jewish writer could have produced this book",[9] then the only way to account for its strong Palestinian traces is upon the assumption that its contents were originally a Palestinian tradition.

It has been set out in the earlier stages of this discussion that Palestinian tradition was not all of one piece. There was a Galilean tradition and a Judean tradition. From which of these sources came the Palestinian basis of the Ephesian tradition? The evidence abounds that it came from the Judean tradition. Therefore the hypothesis that we offer here is that the Synoptic Gospels are the Hellenistic adaptation of a tradition produced chiefly in Galilean Christianity, though with one of the largest sources of Luke derived from Judea, while the Fourth Gospel is based upon an Ephesian tradition, which was an adaptation of tradition produced in Judean Christianity. This would make Matthew and Mark basally Galilean, Luke Galilean and Judean, and John ultimately Judean. There immediately appears a strong objective test of our hypothesis. Are there evidences of any such contact betwen Luke and John as would point toward a common source?

For some time scholars have been observing certain parallels betwen Luke and John, though such a relationsihp has been emphatically disputed by competent scholarship.[10] A careful canvass of the evidence results

---

9 Grant, **Ibid**, p. 215.

10 Cf. Grant, **Journal of Biblical Literature**, vol. 56 (1937), pp. 285-307.

favorably to the hypothesis.[11] Both John and Luke indicate three journeys toward Jerusaiem near the close of Jesus' ministry (Jn. 7:2ff.; 11:7ff.; 12:1ff.; Lu. 9:51; 13:22; 17:11). When Jesus journeyed to the Feast of Tabernacles, six months prior to the crucifixion, John represents him as going there "not publicly, but as it were in secret" (7:10). Luke discloses how he made the journey "in secret": he traveled along the unfrequented Samarian route, a way that Galilean Jews practically never took in going to the feasts at Jerusalem, for reasons quite familiar to the New Testament student (Lu. 9:51,52). Lu. 13:22 indicates the contact of Jesus with towns adjacent to Jerusalem. One such visit could possibly have been the journey to Bethany described in Jn. 11:7ff. After the Feast of Dedication and the raising of Lazarus, according to John, Jesus retired to solitude near the border of Samaria (Jn.11:54). Then after a brief period of absence he returned to Jerusalem. Luke's record combines readily with this account, reporting that Jesus, doubtless in a continuation of the effort to elude his enemies, passed on northward through Samaria into southern Galilee, and came back to Passover along the customary Perean route. "And it came to pass, as he went to Jerusalem, that he passed through the midst of Samaria and Galilee" (Lu. 17:11).

The harmonizing and chronological correlation of the materials of our Gospels is a process which criticism now knows calls for extreme caution, but here the justification is in the convincing nature of the case, for this similarity in general plan of the the two Gospels is supported by

11 A clear summary of the case has been offered by A. T. Robertson, **Harmony of the Gospels**, pp. 276-279.

an abundance of more detailed evidence.

It is noteworthy that Jerusalem holds a decidedly more prominent place in Luke than in either of the other Synoptics. He begins and closes his Gospel in Jerusalem, the childhood of Jesus is linked with Jerusalem (2:41ff.), Jesus went from Jerusalem to the inauguration of his Galilean ministry (4:14), he terminates his Galilean ministry by departing for Jerusalem (9:51), while in Matthew and Mark he goes from his Galilean ministry to "Judea beyond Jordan"(Mt. 19:1; Mk. 10:1).We have already noted three journeys toward Jerusalem near the close of the ministry as recorded by Luke. More than half of the text of Luke's Gospel is devoted to material which is a clear approach to the climax at Jerusalem, and seems to be regarded by Luke as related to Jerusalem and its vicinity. Luke's Passion Narrative and Resurrection Account are more closely related to Jerusalem than is true of Matthew and Mark.

Luke-Acts uses the expression "the Jews" in very much the same way in which it is employed in the Fourth Gospel.[12] This usage reflects a locality in which primitive Christianity was in competition with a most intense form of Judaism, and hence suffering from violent hostility which generated deep prejudice against Judaism as such. No better localization of such reactions could be suggested than Judea. (N.B. I Thes. 2:14,15, where the designation "the Jews" is used in the same way in which John and Luke employ it, and is expressly connected with Judea.)

---

12   Cf. Riddle, **Journal of Religion x, 4, p. 553.**

Luke connects the Galilean ministry most naturally with the "Judean ministry" of John's Gospel by placing the Rejection at Nazareth immediately after Jesus entered Galilee. Upon re-entering Galilee it would be the expected course for him to return first to his home town. He would have been naturally inclined to make Nazareth the center of his Messianic activity: so his establishment of head-quarters at Capernaum is most easily explained in the light of Luke's order of the narrative. Luke fits here quite readily into John. In Lu. 4:23 reference is made to certain things "done in Capernaum", while Luke's account has not indicated any previous contact with Capernaum. The reference is based upon a tradition of a former visit to Capernaum not recorded by Luke. We find such a tradition reflected in Jn. 2:12, where there is brief reference to a sojourn in Capernaum which could plausibly be regarded as belonging to the early ministry. The verse may be the survival of a Judean tradition of such a visit in the early ministry of Jesus. If so, it constitutes a serviceable supplement to Lu. 4:23.[13]

We may note that the healing of the Centurion's Servant is found only in Matthew (8:5ff.) and Luke (7:2ff.). It appears highly probable that this incident is identical with John's narrative of the Healing of the Nobleman's Son (4:46-54). Since the record does not occur in Mark it constitutes another link between the Third and Fourth Gospels. The wide differences between Matthew and Luke make it doubtful that they obtained their narratives at this point directly from the same source. Even their

13 See Macgregor on "Gospel of John" in Moffatt's New Testament Commentary.

records must have been based upon different traditions. We would suggest that Matthew's source was Galilean (from M?), Luke's Judean (through L), and John's Judean-Ephesian.

In the record of the Feeding of the Five Thousand we find the opportunity of a very constructive comparison, for there all four Gospels offer a narrative of the same event. Close examination discloses some interesting contacts between Luke and John in this record. Mark's account is very indistinct as to the locality in which the miracle took place, and would leave the impression that it occurred on the west side of the Lake of Galilee: Luke and John clearly locate it on the east side of the Lake. In Mark the multitudes are represented as gathering from the surrounding towns and villages ($\sigma\upsilon\nu\acute{\epsilon}\delta\rho\alpha\mu\upsilon\nu$): in Luke and John they follow Jesus around the Lake ($\mathring{\eta}\kappa\upsilon\lambda\upsilon\acute{\upsilon}\theta\eta\sigma\alpha\nu$, $\mathring{\eta}\kappa\upsilon\lambda\upsilon\acute{\upsilon}\theta\epsilon\iota$). In Mark it was the "many" ($\pi\upsilon\lambda\lambda\upsilon\acute{\iota}$) who came to Jesus: in Luke and John the "multitudes" ($\mathring{o}\chi\lambda\upsilon\acute{\iota}$, $\mathring{o}\chi\lambda\upsilon\varsigma$) gather. Mark and John agree on $\pi\upsilon\lambda\grave{\upsilon}\varsigma$ $\mathring{o}\chi\lambda\upsilon\varsigma$ at one point (Mk. 6:34; Jn. 6:5). In Mark he "taught them many things" (6:34), while in Luke and John he healed the sick (Lu. 9:11; Jn. 6:2). Luke and John agree with Mark in mentioning the probable cost of buying food sufficient for the multitudes. Matthew omits this item. Mark (6:39) states the fact that Jesus commanded the people to sit down, while Luke and John quote the command, though in different wording. Mark states the number of the multitudes after the feeding: Luke and John state it in connection with the preparation for the feeding. Though taken as a whole Luke is much more similar to Mark in this fourfold record than he is to John, yet his Gospel and John present some contacts which are significant.[14] Surely at this one place alone the phenomena are sufficient to warn us against urging literary dependence of John upon either Luke or Mark. It is better to assume their relations as arising from an ultimate traditional source, with Luke and John standing closer together in the development of the tradition. That is, the tradition behind John's account departed later in its development from the tradition behind Luke's account than from the tradition behind Mark's account. Since Matthew agrees now with Mark, then with Luke, his source must have resulted from a combination of the traditions behind those two. We would propose a hypothetical explanation in the following graph: —

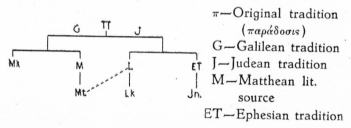

π—Original tradition
    (παράδοσις)
G—Galilean tradition
J—Judean tradition
M—Matthean lit.
    source
ET—Ephesian tradition

The account of the Raising of Lazarus in John is connected with "the village of Mary and her sister Martha" (11:1) in such phraseology as would forcefully imply that these two women were familiar figures in the church life where the tradition originated. Such a situation is of course not conceivable for Ephesus. Both John and Luke (10:38ff.) place the residence of these sisters in Judea. Supposing them to have been two women who

---

14 Per contra see Grant, **Journal of Biblical Literature**, lvi, p. 291.

became prominent in Judean church activities, then it becomes vividly conceivable how a tradition originating there would take for granted familiarity with their names. Then the facts would seem to be these: in Judean Christianity there were two sistres, Martha and Mary, who became familiar figures; certain traditions became connected with their home; both Luke and John drew upon this original Judean tradition, though recording different narratives taken from it. Then Luke and John again converge at their original sources.

In Jn. 12:24,25 we find language which presents a fairly close parallel to Mt. 10:38, 39; 16:24,25; Mk. 8:34, 35; Lu. 9:23,24; 17:33. The passage Lu. 9:23 is parallel with Mk. 8:34,35, and therefore may be regarded as from a Galilean source. But Lu. 17:33 is in Luke's L section, and hence to be ascribed to a Judean source. Then it is highly significant that it is just this form of the saying in Luke which agrees with Jn. 12:25 in differing from Mark. The Lucan version differs considerably from John, but both differ here quite decidedly from Mark, showing independence of the Marcan or Galilean source. Lu. 17:33 is one version of the Judean source, while Jn. 12:25 is a later Ephesian version of the same source. Once more then a common traditional source of Luke and John is suggested, and that traditional source belonging to Judean Christianity.

Assuming that Lu. 22:14-34 and Jn. 13:1-38 are based upon an original authentic tradition, we find that they supplement each other quite effectively. Lu. 22:14-19a may be regarded as a record of events occurring between Jn. 13:1 and 2. Lu. 22:19*b*, 20 is a textual problem to which reference already has been made. Jn. 13:2-11 is a lesson in humility which observation of manifest jealousies among the Twelve had convinced Jesus was needed. Then Lu. 22:21-23 and Jn. 13:21-30 are parallel in substance. Lu. 22:24 indicates the occasion for the lesson of humility described in Jn. 13:2-11, and verses 25 to 30 record teachings which were designed to enforce the lesson. Lu. 22:31-34 and Jn. 13:36-38 are variant traditional accounts of the same incident. Lu. 22:15,16 carries an implication that the Last Supper was not the Passover, as is explicitly represented in Jn. 13:1, 29, etc. Both records have been freely embellished by didactic expansion, especially that of John. Mark and Matthew will be found to vary widely from this reconstruction based upon Luke and John, which suggests that the tradition represented in Luke and John could have come originally from the same group of churches, but Matthew and Mark were separate from them in origin.

In Jn. 18:2 there appears a similiarity to Lu. 22:39 which is significantly supplementary. In Luke we are told that as Jesus retired from Jerusalem at the approach of nightfall, he went "as his custom was" to the Mount of Olives, and it is indicated that, according to custom, the "disciples also followed him". This reveals a general habit of the Master to sojourn, in company with the Twelve, in some convenient resting-place on the slopes of Olivet. There we find a supplementary parallel to John's statement that on the night of the betrayal Judas found Jesus quite readily because he "knew the place: for Jesus oft-times resorted thither with his disciples".

There is no place where all four of the Gospels more nearly agree in an account of the same incident than in the record of Peter's Denial. Here Luke is closer to Mark than he is to John, but at the same time his record more nearly approximates John's than does either of the other two Synoptics. Wherever Luke's account of this incident came from, it was subject to some of the same influences that affected the tradition which furnished an original source for John's Gospel.

There is a vividness of the record of the trial before Pilate in Luke and John which distinguishes them in common from Mark and Matthew. In Matthew's account there are 17 verses, Mark has 15 verses, Luke has 25 and John has 29. Then there is a vividness of detail characterizing Luke and John which distinguishes them in this part of the record from the first two Synoptics. This distinction may be accounted for by the Judean origin of the tradition behind Luke and John, for it was in Judea that memory of details would naturally have been most vivid. Especially does John's record at this point suggest a Judean origin.

It is Luke and John who give us the record of the scars, where the nails were driven through the hands of Jesus—a feature of the Passion Narrative which has ever made forceful appeal to Christian sentiment (Lu. 24:39; Jn. 20:25,27). The terminology and connection are quite different as between the two Gospels, but a common source for the tradition can hardly be doubted.

The instances here observed are illustrative of the many contacts between the Passion Narratives of Luke

and John, and further investigation would disclose yet
others. Vincent Taylor[15] lists the following parallels: —

Jn. 19:4,6 —Lu. 23:14,22
Jn. 13:16   —Lu. 22:26
Jn. 13:29   —Lu. 22:3
Jn. 13:36ff.—Lu. 22:31ff.
Jn. 18:2   —Lu. 22:39
Jn. 18:10   —Lu. 22:50
Jn. 18:38   —Lu. 23:4
Jn. 19:41   —Lu. 23:53

So many agreements could hardly be accidental or co-
incidental, yet it is not possible to suppose that John was
using Luke as a source. A common traditional source
behind both Gospels is the best explanation. And a
common Judean provenance is reflected in the two narratives.[16]

Certainly at this point critical scholarship would not
venture to claim that Luke is related to the same source
as Mark and Matthew. The independence of Luke's
Passion Narrative may be accepted as an established
conclusion of Gospel criticism, for there is practically
unanimous assent of present-day New Testament scholars
to the observation of Vincent Taylor that it has been
"lifted above the realm of mere conjecture as much as
any source-hypothesis is ever likely to be".[17] But while
clearly independent as compared with Matthew and Mark,

15 Op. cit., p. 53.

16 Dean Colwell observes that in the account of the trial of Jesus
John's Gospel "agrees with Luke's very closely", though he sees the reason
for such agreement in a common purpose. The greater reason is probably
to be found in a common source. (John Defends the Gospel, p. 76.)

17 Op. cit., p. 52; Gardner-Smith, op. cit:, pp. 56-72.

Luke exhibits in this part of his record some striking contacts with John.

Contacts have long been noted between the Resurrection Accounts of Luke and John. Especially is it significant that they both present Jerusalem as the scene of the Resurrection appearances. In fact, it is just here in the Resurrection Account that there is found the strongest evidence of two separate streams of tradition, Galilean and Judean. All four Gospels contain in variant forms the experience of the women at the empty tomb. But immediately we meet a striking divergence which cannot plausibly be accounted for by mere personal preferences of the authors. After an initial appearance to the women (Matthew), the first two Synoptists know of no other appearance in Judea, but contemplate the appearance of the risen Christ to his disciples as occurring in Galilee. Luke knows of a promise of post-Resurrection appearance made in Galilee (24:6), but records no actual appearance there. John knows nothing of either promise or appearance in Galilee, but connectes his Resurrection Account wholly with Jerusalem. Of course in this comparison of Resurrection Accounts we are disregarding the appendices of Mark and John, the former having been added by a different hand many years later, and the latter by the hand of the author of the Gospel before it gained general circulation and for reasons unknown.

Details such as the grave cloths figure more largely in Luke and John than in the other two Gospel accounts. There is distinctly less emphasis on the empty tomb in Matthew and Mark than appears in Luke and John. In both Luke and John the earthly contacts of the risen Christ culminate in a promise of the Spirit's advent, an agreement which Gardner-Smith notes in his observation that in both these Gospels "the work of the Church began with the gift of the Holy Spirit".[18]

Again we find an abundance of evidence such as exceeds the limits of reasonable space. Many instances of contact between Luke and John have been noted by other authors which have not been cited here.[19] In view of such abundant evidence we must concur in the verdict of B. H. Streeter that, "John has so much in common with Luke that, if he did *not* use our Third Gospel, we must conclude that John and Luke had a common source, either in the form of a written document or of oral tradition",[20] and we believe there is increasing probability pointing in the direction of a Judean tradition as the common source. Gardner-Smith in his recent work, while his main thesis entails the combing of the details of the Fourth Gospel for all the observable differences from the Synoptics which can justly be claimed, yet recognizes that the parallels between Luke and John are in some places so significant as to point toward the probability "that in some stage of their development the two streams of tradition had been in contact".[21]

It is important to observe that in the main the contacts which appear between Luke and the Fourth Gospel

18 Op. cit., p. 83.

19 Compare for instance Colwell, op. cit., p. 8f.; Streeter, op. cit.; pp. 401-408; Moffatt, Intro. to the Lit. of the N. T., p. 535; Howard, The Fourth Gospel In Recent Criticism and Interpretation, pp. 144-146.

20 Op. cit., p. 396.

21 Op. cit., p. 78.

are in Luke's non-Markan material,[22] excepting the few
fourfold Gospel records, and in his Markan parallels he
frequently shows similarities to John just where he differs
from Mark. This strongly suggestes the influence upon
Luke of a source which supplied the traditional basis of
the Fourth Gospel. The hypothetical explanation of this
phenomenon lies upon its surface. Luke and John are
both related to a tradition which was developed originally
in Judea. The mutual relation of the two sources to Judea
appears at every turn. The interest is Judean, the setting
is Judean, the prevailing viewpoint is Judean. The only
effective way to refute the theory of the Judean origin of
these two kindred traditions would be to prove that there
was no Judean tradition, for if a Judean tradition existed
it is certainly reflected here.

But it is further to be recognized that the differences
between Luke and John are more pronounced than the
similarities. This could result from the fact that the
Judean tradition behind the Fourth Gospel passed through
the processes of traditional propagation in Ephesian
Christianity, whereby it became a distinctive Ephesian
tradition. Hence there appears the basis for a strong
inference in favor of a Judean origin of the Ephesian
tradition recorded in the Fourth Gospel. Streeter finds
evidence in the Gospel which leads him to the opinion
that it "may possibly rest on a Jerusalem tradition".[23]

An important clue to the origin of the Ephesian tradition is furnished in the fact that Luke and John recog-

22 The source designated as L. Cf. Grant, **Journal of Biblical Literature,**
vol. lvi, p. 304.

23 **Op. cit., p. 403**

nize a contact of Jesus with Samaria which is not known
to the other two Gospels (Lu. 9:52; 10:33; 17:11; Jn.
4:4). Luke's interest in Samaria is especially evident in
Acts. Frequently critical students of Acts have recognized a sort of geographical outline of the book in Ac.
1:8. This verse discloses the early stages in the spread
of the Christian religion, significantly omitting Galilee.
Jerusalem is represented as the fountainhead of the
stream of gospel influence, and the second stage is "all
Judea and Samaria". Thus Samaritan Christianity is
intimately associated with Judea. Then the cause spread
to the Gentile world, "the uttermost part of the earth",
from this basis. We cannot justly assume that the
Galilean disciples had no part in the extension of Christianity to the Gentile world. We must rather conclude
that we have before us in Acts a tradition which was not
informed as to the Galilean mission. The early chapters
of Acts present an account of apostolic preaching as
preserved in a Judean tradition. It contemplates the
gospel as going from Judea and Samaria out to the
Gentile world. The Gentile mission thus promoted embraced Ephesus. Then we may conclude that the early
Christian tradition planted in Ephesus originated in the
churches of Judea and Samaria. This will satisfactorily
explain the dominant Judean and Samaritan interest in
John, L and Ac. i-xii.

These highly plausible inferences may be reinforced
by notice of the intimate relation of Christianity in
Cæsarea and Ephesus. We regard such relations as
reasonably inferred from three considerations.

(1) Obviously Cæsarea was the natural point of contact for Ephesus with Palestinian Christianity. There was constant transportation and communication between the two points. It was at Cæsarea that Paul landed toward the close of his second missionary tour when he went up to Jerusalem "and saluted the church" (Ac. 18:22). Galilean Christianity would touch the Gentile world through Antioch and plant its tradition there; Judean Christianity would touch the Gentile world through Cæsarea and Ephesus, and spread its tradition along that route. In L and Ac. i-xii is represented Judean tradition as planted in Cæsarea; in John we have Judean tradition as transplanted in Ephesus.

(2) There is an ancient tradition which carries a reflection that the evangelist Philip and his daughters settled in Heirapolis late in the Apostolic Age.[24] They would naturally have moved to this destination through Cæsarea and Ephesus. We know by specific record that they dwelt at one time in Cæsarea (Ac. 21:8). Therefore Ephesus is the only link we must supply by inference, and the inference is highly plausible when all the facts are considered as to transportation routes, natural lines of communication, dominant centers of Christian influence, etc. Philip and his daughters were but following the rather fixed channels through which Christian life flowed from Jerusalem into the Græco-Roman world. Jerusalem Cæsarea, Ephesus, were obviously natural points of progress.

(3) The third Gospel incorporates a source (L) which

24 Cf. Streeter, **The Primitive Church**, pp. 37, 60.

is manifestly of Judean origin, and at the same time shows traces of Samaritan tradition. This Samaritan influence would impinge upon Judean tradition at Cæsarea. If Luke the companion of Paul was the author of the third Gospel, as many of the best scholars believe, then he was also the author of Acts, and was on this thesis unquestionably with Paul during much of the time of his imprisonment at Cæsarea. Here he would have had ample opportunity to form the contacts which would have enabled him to secure the material included in the L section of his Gospel. And, perhaps more important, there could have been at this time created in him the personal interest in Judean-Samaritan Christianity which would have influenced him in giving such a large place in his Gospel to such material. Assuming this to be a true representation of the facts (and this writer heartily believes that it is) we have again the same line of connection, Jerusalem, Cæsarea, Hellenism. There is perhaps a course of development here more important in the study of New Testament history and literature than we have formerly realized.

These lines of connection are destined to become clearer and more strongly supported as investigation proceeds. Such evidence will help to confirm the view that in the Fourth Gospel we have the record of a tradition which arose in Judea and Samaria, passed through Cæsarea to Ephesus, and was remolded and adapted to its developing needs by Ephesian Christianity. The secure establishment of such a hypothesis would remove much confusion from the problem of the origin of the Fourth Gospel.

As we come to the conclusion of this discussion, there is yet one more question to be raised. Granted the thesis which we have just delineated is true, what advantages have we gained in the study of the Fourth Gospel? We believe there are at least five points at which we can claim advancement in the light of such an explanation of its origin.

1. Some baffling problems, such as the relation of the chronology of John to that of the Synoptic Gospels, the apparent disarrangement in the text of the Gospel, the difference from and similarity to the Synoptic Gospels, with many details of interpretation in specific difficult passages, have found a solution. The author himself has found his thesis providing a helpful predicate for interpretation at many points. Previous critics and interpreters have frequently pointed in the direction our thesis has taken as offering possible solutions for difficult problems, which leads us to believe that more definite and detailed investigation and application will lead to highly fruitful results.

2. We believe our hypothesis has relieved at least some of the strain on the vexed question of authorship. If the tradition recorded in the Gospel goes back to Palestinian sources and eyewitness testimony, conservative scholars will not feel so keenly the possible loss to the factual foundations of evangelical Christian faith in surrendering the apostolic authorship; and if the question of authorship thus becomes intermediate and secondary

the liberal scholar will not tend to be so vehement in his denials of apostolic authorship. Authorship will have less bearing upon the question of the character of the material which composes the Gospel. That question must be settled chiefly on other considerations. If such a new predicate has successfully been introduced, then we can be calm in the discussion of the problem of Johannine authorship. We feel that this is no small gain!

The hypothesis here submitted throws into entirely new perspective the question of authorship. If the contentions offered above are true, they automatically dissolve most of the internal arguments long urged in support of the tradition of apostolic authorship. A strong sequence of inferences has been adduced from internal evidence which made the theory of apostolic authorship appear quite plausible. This train of logically consecutive inferences has been constructed thus: The author of the Fourth Gospel was a Jew; that Jew was a Palestinian Jew; that Palestinian Jew was an eye-witness; that eye-witness was a personal disciple of Jesus; that disciple was the Apostle John, the son of Zebedee.[1]

That the author was a Jew has been infered for the distinctly Jewish flavor of much of the material; but a Palestinian tradition would possess such Jewish characteristics irrespective of the author who recorded it. That the author was a Pelestinian Jew was thought to be attested by the vivid local coloring of the book, and the Semitic traces in the language; but these phenomena are

1 Cf. Peak, **Critical Introduction to the New Testament**, pp. 194-211; Dods, **Expositor's Greek Testament**, vol. i, p. 665; Reynolds, "The Gospel of John", **Hasting's Dictionary of the Bible** (1899), vol. ii, pp. 702-705.

sufficiently explained by an original Aramaic tradition, even if the author had been a Gentile who never saw Palestine. The many very impressive evidences of eye-witness testimony which have been discerned in the book may be explained by a tradition which came originally from those who were eye-witnesses, even if such a tradition had been written down by an author who was not living at the time of the events. The reflection of the intimate knowledge of the experiences and associates of Jesus which have been regarded as proving that the author was a personal disciple, are to be accounted for by the fact that the original tradition was formulated under the influence of personal disciples of Jesus; so the author may never have seen the Master. Thus if the hypothesis posited in this discussion stands, the force of these arguments for internal evidence of apostolic authorship vanishes. It also eliminates the occasion for the "pilgrim at Jerusalem" of Streeter and others.[2]

3. The historical value of the Fourth Gospel is inevitably enhanced. If the material which it contains has as its original basis a Palestinian tradition and reminiscenses of the original disciples of Jesus, then its records are obviously much more trustworthy than would be a midhrashic narrative produced largely out of the fancy of a Christian Gnostic at the end of the first century. The teaching material recorded, though not a verbal reproduction of the Aramaic sayings of Jesus, yet reflects the faith of a group of Asian churches in what could rightfully be considered the message of their Lord. It could then be regarded as the import of his original message

2 The Four Gospels, p. 419.

"profoundly influenced by the environment of the growing church with its increasing perception of the significance of the exalted Jesus".[3] If the premise here employed is acceptable, then the narrative elements of the Fourth Gospel are based upon actual occurrences in the experience of Jesus, though scholars will still vary widely as to how far traditional processes had modified and embellished these narratives.

4. As it is true that the Palestinian churches are mirrored in the records of the Synoptic Gospels,[4] so the Asain churches of the last quarter of the first century are speaking to us between the lines of the Fourth Gospel. Their problems and practices, their life and thought are behind every one of its pages. Undoubtedly these elements are woven into a relatively original production of the author, but what he presents has been derived from the heart and mind of Ephesian Christianity, and reflects the life of Ephesian Christianity.

In the Synoptic Gospels we see Jesus through the eyes of the Palestinian churches; in the Fourth Gospel we see him through the eyes of the Asian churches. This is the nearest we can ever hope to get to the historical Jesus. Critical scholarship will continue to deliberate and debate over the inferences relative to the actual historical Jesus which may be legitimately derived from these sources, and the evidences for and against their trustworthiness, but it can never be more than conjecture when we seek to get behind the tradition of the primitive Chris-

3   Hopwood, op. cit., p. 18.

4   Kundsin, in Grant, Form Criticism, p. 81.

tian churches. Here only can we discern the Founder of our religion. I for one would not ask for a better way to view him. As a scientific student I shall join my contemporaries in tracing every possible thread that may lead us back to the Jesus of history; as a worshiper at the throne of grace divine I shall continue in the fellowship and faith of the teaching Messiah of Palestinian Christianity and the redeeming Christ of the Ephesian church. It enriches my religious life far more to contemplate him in the simple light of their religious convictions than in the rather shadowy perspective of modern critical scholarship. The findings of scholarship unquestionably have their great value in the progress of knowledge among men; but the simple faith of the apostolic churches aids me more in the progress of my soul toward God.

5. In the light of the hypothesis here proposed we have the basis for a more satisfactory solution for the problem of the authorship of the Johannine epistles. The best Greek scholarship has all but unanimously pronounced in favor of the unity of authorship of the Gospel and epistles of John. Yet there is a slight difference between the Greek of I John and that of the Gospel. This may now quite plausibly be accounted for by the hypothesis that the epistles are the natural freehanded style of the writer, while the style of the Gospel is influenced by the tradition he is using. We have an instructive parallel in the work of Luke. In Luke's Gospel we have one style, in Acts i-xii a slightly different style, and in Acts xiii-xxviii still another slight modificaton in style. This is of course to be accounted for by the influence of different sources upon the style of Luke. Probably in the "we"-sections

we have the original, spontaneous style of Luke, just as in the epistles we have the normal style of John.

If we regard I Jn. 2:7-11; 3:11-16; 4:7-21 as a practical exposition of the tradition recorded in Jn. 13:34-35 we have laid a predicate for a better understanding of the difference in mode of expression. The style in the Gospel is crisp, concise, pointed; that in the epistle is elaborate, involved, expansive: exactly the sort of difference which naturally obtains between original statement and exposition. We believe that detailed application of this hypothesis at this point will increase its plausibility.

There is yet one other question in the mind of the devout evangelical student who may have read these pages. How may we harmonize all these theories of human origins with the doctrine of divine inspiration? We will have no difficulty at this point if we will contemplate the redemptive purposes of God overshadowing the entire process. In these historical and literary developments we have but the earthly agencies and methods employed by the divine Spirit in giving us the Gospel records. Scientific interpretation seeks to discern and interpret the phenomena of human development and activity in the production of the Gospel text; Christian faith discerns, hovering over it all, the directing and motivating presence of the Spirit of God, as he makes gracious provision for the religious needs and progress of all generations to come. Those who wish to stop with the scientific investigation are at liberty to do so: some of us prefer to look farther, and find rich satisfaction of

heart and strength of character in the faith that the redemptive hand of God was present in it all.

The process of ancient literary development which
issued in the production of the Fourth Gospel is a part
of the most marked and beneficial development in the
religious history of mankind. It was by this process that
the Messianic ideal and hero of an obscure group of
devout Jewish religionists in Palestine became the Teacher,
Example and Reedemer of the world. It lifted Jesus from
the obscurity of a martyred Messianic agitator in the re-
mote province of Judea to the place of primal factor in the
upward progress of the human race, for had no evangelic
tradition been formulated, or no evangelic record transcribed, Jesus of Nazareth could never have been the
Christ of Christian faith, and it is as the Christ of Christian faith that he has conferred his incomparable blessing
on mankind. Some may regard these developments as
but the expanding delusions of a deceived religious cult,
but we are pleased to see in them the unfolding plan of
a spiritual redemption, designed by the love of an eternal
God.

EVANGELIC DEVELOPMENT

The diagram on the opposite page summarizes the
hypothesis offered in this book in explanation of the
sources of our canonical Gospels. Designations that are
underscored indicate oral sources.

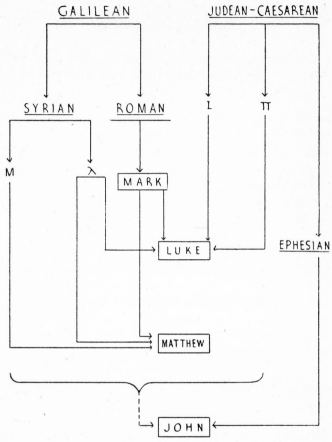

M—Source of Matthew's independent material.

λ—Source of discourse material common to Matthew and
     Luke.

L—Source of Luke x-xviii.

π—Source of Luke's Passion Narrative and Resurrection
     Account.

   These four sources are presumably documentary.

APPENDIX

THE TRADITIONAL TITLE OF THE FOURTH GOSPEL

The Fourth Gospel, along with the other three, is essentially anonymous. We may assume with a high degree of assurance that the titles attached to our four Gospels did not have as their original primary design the identification of the author, but rather the differentiation of the several documents. When the four evangelic writings were collected and used in the churches as a fourfold Gospel "canon", each needed a distinguishing title. Hence they came to be designated, "According to Matthew", "According to Mark", etc. Here κατά does not necessarily mean, "by the hand of", but more probably, "on the authority of". That is, in devising these titles the early churches may have used either the name of the one who composed the document or of the one who was known to have been vitally connected with the origin of its material.

Of course there was some reason for the selection of the several titles, and the most rational understanding of the development requires that we suppose that some fact which they believed to be connected with the origin of each Gospel prompted the churches in selecting these titles. It is hardly conceivable that they devised a title at random, just as a matter of "naming" a Gospel. The two possible motives named above commend themselves to conservative critical judgment as the most natural reasons for the selection of the four titles. Accepting this hypothesis, we would consider it probable that the first and fourth Gospels derived their titles from the chief apostolic influence in their traditional sources, and the second and third were named for their authors. Such designations would of course be according to the prevailing opinion in the churches of the first half of the second century: the accuracy of that opinion is rightfully subject to question.

It so happens that in the case of Mark's Gospel we have an early second century tradition relative to both the author and the chief apostolic influence affecting its traditional source. This is the well-known tradition reported by Papias that Mark secured his material largely from his familiarity with the preaching of Peter.

At this point we must be very careful to have in mind the proper conception of what the "preaching of Peter" meant in that age. If we do not exercise special care at this point we will find ourselves with a picture in mind of Peter standing in a carpeted pulpit, with a mahogany or oak desk before him, delivering a formal sermon with its conventional firstly, secondly and thirdly, and interspersing a few anecdotes about Jesus as illustrative material. This is wholly alien to the true picture, which should vizualize Peter standing—or more likely seated, since he was a Palestinian Jew—in the midst of a small group of Christians gathered in a Roman home, teaching them the παράδοσις as he had slowly formulated it in memory with the help of his apostolic and missionary associates.

Whence came this Petrine tradition? What was its original provenance? To answer this question requires that we trace the apostolic activities of Peter. Since the

place of tradition in his experience is signiffcantly illustrative of Gospel development in general, we offer a brief
sketch of what we believe to be, toward the end of his
life, his probable career. We know from the second
chapter of Galatians that Peter journeyed from Jerusalem
to Antioch. We believe that the date of Galatians places
it just prior to Ac.15:1ff., and that Peter's visit described
in Gal. 2:11ff. came before the Jerusalem Council. Peter's
status in the church at Jerusalem was permanently im-
paired by his ministry to the house of Cornelius, and after
his experience at Antioch and his aggressive defence of
Paul in the Jerusalem Council, his relations became more
severely strained and he was entirely displaced by James
the brother of Jesus.

Having lost his leadership in the rigid church at
Jerusalem, the natural move for Peter to make next was
to Galilee, his home country and a situation possessing a
more liberal mind than Judea. We believe that an un-
written chapter in the apostolic labors of Simon Peter
belongs to Galilee. While there he would have been inevitably the most influential factor in the formation of a
Galilean tradition. This then would be the tradition
which he carried out to the Hellenistic world. We believe
some such developments to have taken place. That Peter
engaged widely in missionary activities is clearly reflected
in I Co. 9:4. His final residence in Rome is attested by
a combination of evidence which most scholars regard as
convincing. Then we conclude that he introduced into
Rome the Galilean tradition, and it became the basic
element in the tradition recorded in Mark's Gospel.

A very similar apostolic experience is probably in the

background of the first Gospel. It seems that the Apostle Matthew labored for a season in Judea and Galilee, and then (around 50 A.D.?) settled in Syria, perhaps at Antioch. He too was deeply imbued with the Galilean tradition, and promoted it in Syria. Accepting the testimony of Papias, we would conclude that Matthew himself began the process of committting this tradition to writing. If the Papias tradition is true,[1] and there appears no sufficient reason for rejecting it, then Matthew must have ministered in Syria. There would have been no conceivable occasion for producing a written record of the sayings of Jesus in Palestine, for Palestinian Jews did not use the written page but depended wholly on oral transmission. Only in Syria would Matthew have produced a document of sayings in any language that could be described as Ἑβραΐδι. That Jews of that region might have used a Semitic document is attested by the production and circulation of Josephus' first edition of his *War of the Jews*. After Matthew's *Logia* the literary process continued until, with the conflation of Mark and another narrative document with Matthew's document of sayings, the Greek Gospel of Matthew was produced.

The Gospel of Luke seems to have resulted from a process of development which was unique in the field of gospel writing. The time and place of its production are very much in obscurity, and the method was more nearly that of Greek literary effort than the simple recording of tradition. It is in reality Volume One of a quasi-historical work of two volumes, produced much on the order of Greek history writing. It has no single distinct strain of

---

1 Cf. Lightfoot, **Apostolic Fathers**, p. 517.

apostolic tradition as a chief basis. Like Greek historical works it is named for its author.

Our conjectural reconstruction of the traditional sources of Mark and Matthew furnishes a suggestion for an approach to the origin of John. When the siege of Jerusalem drove the Christians out of the city, the Apostle John took refuge in the Hellenistic world. He followed the beaten trail already established between Judean Christianity and the Gentile world — through Cæsarea to Ephesus. In Ephesus he found already established a tradition which had its roots in Judea. Supplementing, modifying and further developing this offspring of Judean tradition, the Apostle John, in normal fulfillment of the recognized apostolic function, became the dominant factor in the Ephesian tradition. Thus the Ephesian tradition became also the Johannine tradition, and the written Gospel which recorded it became the "Gospel According to John".

In the light of the standard tradition of the Church this hypothesis has strong support, but a serious difficulty stands in the way of it. In the last half century new evidence has been brought to light which indicates that the Apostle John suffered matyrdom in the seventh decade of the first century, before the siege of Jerusalem. But we must observe that this evidence suffers greatly from close scrutiny. It consists chiefly of a supposed testimony of Papias.

This "Papias Tradition" witnessing to the early matyrdom of the Apostle John is attested by two literary fragments which came to light in the latter part of the past century. The first was a *Chronicon* of a certain Georgius Hamartolus, an obscure monk of the ninth century. The full text of the fragment reads as follows:

> Then after Domitian, Nerva reigned one year, who, having recalled John from the Island, permitted him to live at Ephesus. Being at that time the only one of the twelve disciples surviving, after having compiled his Gospel he was honored with martyrdom. For Papias, bishop of Heirapolis, being a personal associate of the same, in the second book of his "Sayings of the Lord", says that he was slain by the Jews, fulfilling clearly with his brother the prediction of Christ concerning them and their own confession and undertaking for him. For when the Lord said to them, "Are ye able to drink of the cup of which I shall drink?" and they willingly consented and agreed: "My cup", he says, "ye shall drink, and with the baptism with which I am baptized shall ye be baptized". And so it came to pass, for it was impossible for God to lie. And thus also the much learned Origen in his commentary on Matthew maintains—that is, that John met martyrdom, contending that he had learned this from the successors of the apostles. And then indeed also the well-informed Eusebius in his Church History says, "Thomas received by lot Parthia, but John Asia, among whom also he lived out and culminated his life in Ephesus".[2]

The confusion and contradiction of this document is obvious on the face of it. Some of us are unwilling to impeach Irenæus in favor of such testimony. True, Irenæus does sometimes evidently garble the facts and contradict himself, but nowhere in any such bald and absurd manner as this document. When we have the entire text of the fragment before us we find certain striking phenomena standing out quite boldly.

(1) The writer was evidently very much confused in his own understanding of history. Opening with an unqualified declaration that John was recalled from exile on Patmos by the Emperor Nerva, and that he thereafter compiled his Gospel, the testimony is added that he met martyrdom. When? Quite evidently after his exile and the composition of his Gospel. Then in support of the fact of his martyrdom, the testimony of Papias is added that he was killed by the Jews, linking his death with that of his brother James. Such connections would seem to indicate his death several decades before the time of Nerva. Then the document closes with a testimony, authenticated by the support of Eusebius, that John lived out his later life and died in Ephesus. It is exceedingly doubtful that Georgius recognized that the supposed testimony of Papias contradicted the current tradition of John's residence and death at Ephesus. If so, average intelligence could hardly be ascribed to him, writing into a single paragraph such glaring contradictions. He certainly meant to represent that John died at Ephesus at the hands of the Jews after the beginning of Nerva's reign, and after having written the Gospel ascribed to him. Surely this is confirmed by his claim that John was a personal associate of Papias.

(2) The writer of this fragment garbles and glaringly misinterprets the remarks of Origen relative to the martyrdom of John. What Origen actually said was, "The sons of Zebedee did certainly drink the cup and were baptised with the baptism, since Herod killed James, the

brother of John, with the sword, and the Emperor of the Romans, as tradition records, banished John to the Island of Patmos, for approving the word of truth with his testimony. John himself hands down in the Apocalypse . . . the circumstances of his martyrdom".[3] Clearly Origen knew of no such tradition of Papias, or he would have mentioned it in this connection. Georgius has totally distorted his meaning. Such rank misrepresentation of Origen leads us to hesitate in following him on the testimony of Papias. How may we know that he did not misconstrue Papias? In fact he did, by any sort of rational understanding we might have of what Papias actually said.

(3) The writer frankly betrays his motive in adducing this supposed testimony of Papias. He feels that such a view is indispensable to faith in the infallibility of the prediction of Jesus, as recorded in Mark 10:39. It is his conviction that God, incarnate in Christ, would be guilty of falsehood unless we suppose that this prophecy had a rigidly literal fulfillment.

His observation at this point is thought by many critics to contain a subtle implication which really strengthens the testimony he claims to reproduce from Papias. It is urged that this prophecy would not have survived had it not been authenticated by literal fulfillment. But this contention loses much of its force when we remember that the prediction had been a fixed part of tradition for more than thirty years before John is supposed, on the basis of the "Papias Tradition", to

3 Quoted by Nunn, The Son of Zebedee, p. 17.

have been slain by the Jews, and had been for another thirty years recorded in Mark's Gospel before John's death according to established tradition. It is not likely that the prediction would have been deleted after it had been so long a part of the tradition and the Gospel text, even if it had failed of literal fulfillment.

And it is to be further considered that this passage presented no greater difficulty as to fulfillment than Mt. 16:28 and 24:34, and these prophecies were not suppressed. They may certainly be regarded as "sufficient evidence that the sayings of Jesus were preserved in the Gospel because they were remembered, not because they were framed afterwards to fit events in history".[4] The fact is that we have no objective reason for taking it for granted that a tradition of prophecy would have been suppressed if it appeared not to attain to literal fulfillment. It is much more likely that the "Papias Tradition" was devised to explain this prediction of Jesus, than that the actual martydom of John preserved the prophecy. The former development would be more in line with the manifest tendencies of the early Christian mind.

This bit of evidence, with so many difficulties involved in it, would doubtless never have impressed such fairminded scholars as Charles, Streeter, Moffatt, and Grant had there not appeared what has been regarded as strong confirmation in the form of documentary witness apparently based upon testimony much earlier than the time of Georgius Hamartolus. Among the DeBoor *Texte und Untersuchungen* was published a

---

4 Howard, **The Fourth Gospel in Recent Criticism and Interpretation,** p. 249.

fragment which competent scholars have believed to be from an abridgement of a "History of Christianity" by one Philip of Side. When the full text of the testimony is examined the strength of its confirmation is greatly diminished. Here is the text in full.

Papias, bishop of Hierapolis, being a hearer of John the divine, wrote five treatises on "The Sayings of the Lord", in which, in making a list of the apostles, after Peter and John, Philip and Thomas and Matthew, he included in the list of the disciples of the Lord Aristion and another John, whom he called the "Elder". So some think that to this John belong the two short or general epistles, which are published in the name of John, on the ground that the ancients only accept the first epistle. Some also falsely ascribe to him the Apocalypse. And Papias also errs concerning the millenium and Irenæus after him. In his second book Papias says that John the divine and James his brother were slain by the Jews. This said Papias told as reported by the daughters of Philip that Barnabas, who was also nicknamed Justus, being challenged by the unbelievers, having drunk a potion in the name of Christ, was preserved unharmed. Then he also tells about other wonders, especially that one about the mother of Manaim who was raised from the dead; concerning those raised from the dead by Christ, that they lived until the time of Hadrian.[5]

So similar is this document in its contradictions and distortions to that ascribed to Georgius Hamartolus that one could almost fancy that there had been collusion between the two writers. Together they seem to present a sort of parody on tradition. But there is no question

5 Lightfoot, op. cit., p. 518f.

that both documents were written in perfect sincerety of purpose, and in full confidence that they were accurately recording history. Each had clearly a serious interest to promote in what he was writing. Like the former fragment, this one presents difficulties which cannot escape our notice.

(1) An important element in its strength is supposed to lie in the fact that is was based on a work which was produced by Philip of Side as early as the fifth century. But of this we cannot be sure. The origin of the fragment is largely in obscurity. And even if it came ultimately from Philip of Side, that ancient worthy himself was not regarded as a very reliable authority.[6] We hesitate to lay aside Eusebius of Cæsarea and rely in preference on Philip of Side.

(2) Like its companion witness, this fragment involves a contradiction. It begins by attesting the survival of John to the time of Polycarp and Papias, which would bring his career down near the end of the first century, yet the writer evidently means to associate the martydom of John with that of James, on the supposition that they were contiguous in time as well as circumstances. Yet he fails to testify specifically that the supposed death of John at the hands of the Jews occurred prior to his traditional period of residence at Ephesus. The immediate association of his death with that of his brother James carries such an implication, but in deference to the intelligence of the writer we must urge that he was not conscious of the implication. He is blending two strains of tradition which are in reality mutually contra-

[6] Nunn, op. cit., p. 12.

dictory. Which strain is the more reliable? We cannot sincerely reply otherwise than that it is the one which holds the stronger support from other traditional sources. Plausible rebuttals may be found against this answer, but it has an intrinsic strength which will be difficult to overthrow, and which we believe is destined to prevail, unless stronger confirmation is found for the "Papias Tradition".

We would not ignore confirmation which is offered from another source. It is believed that supporting evidence may be found in the ancient church calendars. But when one examines closely for their historical accuracy these old church calendars, he fails to be greatly impressed with their support. Religious sentiment figured far more largely in their compilation than did historical authencity or chronological accuracy. One of the most ancient of these ancient calendars, and one on which greatest reliance is reposed as a support of the "Papias Tradition", is embraced in a Syriac martyrology of the fourth century. It gives the death of Stephen, the first of the martyrs, the day after Christmas, then James and John together on December 27, followed by Peter and Paul on December 28. How accomodating of these sainted apostles and apostolic leaders to effect their demise at just the right time to fit in at such an appropiate date in the later Christian calendar as the first three days after Christmas! The utterly baseless invention of these anniversary dates is too palpable to need refutation. Then a Carthaginian martyrology of a century later associates John the Baptist with the Apostle James on December 27. This, however, was an unaccepted departure from standard practice in the churches.[7]

It is to be observed that the almost feverishly eager effort to prove the early martyrdom of the Apostle John is invariably connected with arguments against the apostolic authorship of the Fourth Gospel. This leaves an inescapable impression of bias. And as a matter of fact, the strained effort is not justified by the requirements of the case. The critics do not need to kill off the aged Apostle to keep him from writing the Gospel which tradition has ascribed to him. Other considerations weigh heavily enough against that conclusion. To mention one by way of illustration: If the Apostle John, the erstwhile fisherman of Aramaic speaking Galilee, had written the Gospel, it would probably have presented the most awkward Greek of the New Testament, instead of the most typically smooth Koine'. The Greek of the Fourth Gospel is simple, but it flows with a sublime grace and consistency. Greek teachers all agree that it provides the best text in the New Testament for teaching the language to beginners. The one who wrote it was native to it. In view of such considerations as this, we may without alarm permit the humble Apostle John to live out his complete traditional career and die in peace at Ephesus.

There is yet another consideration, however, which we must frankly face. It is strange that we hear so little of the Apostle John in the first half of the second century. This fact, however, must be very greatly magnified to out-weigh the growing accumulation of evidence from A.

7 Nunn, op. cit., p. 46f.

D. 140 on. It is quite easy to place too much strain on
the argument from silence. Furthermore, we must be
careful not to gag the witnesses so that we may draw
inferences from their silence. Controversy has a tendency
to produce extreme methods.

There is no very sound reason why an entirely unprejudiced criticism should reject the testimony of
Andreas of Cæsarea that Papias ascribed the Apocalypse
to John.[8] Certainly any John could have written it, but
John the son of Zebedee fits the case quite well. And
such a position raises as effective a barrier between him
and the Fourth Gospel as would his early matyrdom, for
only intensely apologetic interests can bring a competent
Greek scholar to conclude that the same hand could have
written the Greek of both the Fourth Gospel and the
Apocalypse. When Andreas wrote his commentary on
the Apocalypse the writings of Papias were undoubtedly
still extant, so it would have been folly, not to say pure
perfidy, for him to have claimed the support of Papias
in his contention for apostolic authorship when he knew
there really existed no such testimony. And it is be-
wilderingly strange that Papias, who was a contemporary of the writer of Revelation, should have had a confused and erroneous notion about the authorship of the
book. It requires the towering genius of a Benjamin W.
Bacon to solve this problem![9]

Justin Martyr was converted to Christianity at
Ephesus, where the Apocalypse undoubtedly attained
its initial circulation. He was converted about 130 A.D.,

8   Lightfoot, op. cit., p. 520.
9   The Fourth Gospel in Research and Debate, pp. 104ff., 176.; The
Gospel of the Hellenists, pp. 21, 22.

thirty-five years after the book of Revelation was written. It seems hardly probable that Ephesian Christianity would have developed a legendary theory of authorship in so short time. These facts should be very earnestly considered before we summarily discard the reliability of Justin's testimony, given in such specific terms in his *Dialogue,* lxxxi, "And further, there was a certain man with us, whose name was John, one of the Apostles of Christ, who prophesied by a revelation that was made to him, that those who believed in our Christ would dwell a thousand years in Jerusalem; and that thereafter the general, and in short, the eternal resurrection and judgment of all men would likewise take place". To set aside such explicit testimony under such conditions could be justified only by the very strongest contrary evidence, unless one agrees with the verdict that it has been "demonstrated that the second-century tradition is devoid of historical value".[10] With all our tender regard for the sacred memory of the author of that statement, we must emphatically pronounce it the expression of a radical anti-traditional prejudice.

It is self-evident that if the Apostle John was the writer of the Apocalypse, then of necessity he lived until the time of Domitian, for New Testament scholarship is all but unanimous in dating Revelation during Domitian's reign.

The most abundant and emphatic testimony in the second century to the late survival of the Apostle John is that of Irenæus. Be it admitted without hesitation that his testimony is fraught with so many complicated prob-

10 Bacon, **Gospel of the Hellenists,** p. 48.

lems that one cannot feel perfectly secure about its value; however, when one contemplates such a careful, exhaustive and unprejudiced review of the Irenæus evidence as that presented by F. G. Lewis' dissertation on *The Irenaeus Testimony to the Fourth Gospel* (Chicago, 1908), he finds himself impressed with a new conviction that a cautious criticism will not lightly dismiss such evidence as having no weight in the final decision relative to the origin of the Fourth Gospel. Such testimony as that contained in the letter of Irenæus to Florinus[11] presents strong intrinsic merit. It is quite the fashion in critical circles, and not without cause, to impeach the accuracy, or even the veracity, of Irenæus; but it is hardly conceivable that he would have written a falsehood to a great Christian contemporary, under the guise of reminding him of facts with which he is supposed to be relatively familiar. In such a connection Florinus would of course have recognized prevarication on sight; so it is hard to believe that a man of Irenæus' intelligence, waiving the whole question of his honesty, would so fatally have invalidated his entire appeal to Florinus.

The earliest testimony we have to the apostolic authorship of the Fourth Gospel is in the form of a defence of that position. Canon Streeter finds in this fact serious grounds for questioning the validity of the tradition.[12] But there is another implication involved. A denial inevitably involves a prior claim. No one would have been disputing the apostolic authorship of the Fourth Gospel unless first there had been a claim for

11   Eusebius, "Church History", 5:20:5, 6.
12   Four Gospels, p. 437.

such authorship. The belief in Johannine authorship preceded the objection to it, even as the objection must necessarily have preceded the defence. This self-evident inference means that in the last quarter of the second century there was a widely prevalent belief practically throughout the Christian world that John the Apostle, son of Zebedee, wrote the Fourth Gospel. This belief finds positive and direct attestation in the Muratorian Fragment, Theophilus of Antioch, Ptolemy the Gnostic, Polycrates, *et alii*.[13]

Such strong traditional evidence cannot be cast aside. It is difficult to explain its existence unless the Apostle John had some connection with the Fourth Gospel. Conservative criticism would probably persist in abiding by its verdict of apostolic authorship were it not for the fact that the external evidence for the authorship of Revelation is earlier and intrinsically stronger than that for the Gospel. The differences between the two books are too radical to admit a view of common authorship. Hence we feel constrained to assign the Apocalypse to the Apostle John and look elsewhere for the hand that wrote the Gospel.

A hypothesis is needed which will account for the strong testimony of late second century tradition, and also the wide variance between the Gospel and Apocalypse. Then there are other difficulties in the way of accepting the apostolic authorship of the Gospel the detailed treatment of which cannot be included in this paper. A rational explanation may be found in the

Criticism of the Fourth Gospel, pp. 99ff.; Eusebius, "Church History", 3:31:3.
13 Ezra Abbott, Authorship of the Fourth Gospel, pp. 58, 60; Sanday,

theory that the Apostle John was the chief apostolic factor in moulding the tradition recorded in the Fourth Gospel, making it in that sense the "Gospel According to John", and that another John who had been a personal disciple of Jesus did the writing.[14] This explanation is greatly strengthened if we allow the supposition that both Johns lived at Ephesus near the end of the first century. Since Papias mentiones an "Elder John" as distinct for the Apostle by that name, it becomes easy to identify him with the "Elder" who wrote the second and third epistle of John, and *ex hypothesi* the first epistle and the Gospel. We believe that this is the most plausible hypothesis that can be offered for the composition of the Fourth Gospel in the light of the evidence which we now possess.

This theory calls out of the shadows that rather tenuous and much debated figure of Papias', "John the Presbyter". Quite obviously he fits well into the hypothesis as "the other John" who was a disciple of Christ, and hence very easily confused with the son of Zebedee in late second century Christian tradition. But plausibility is not proof. To begin with there is obscurity and ambiguity in the statement of Papias, which reads as follows:

> And then furthermore if anyone came who had been a follower of the elders, I would make inquiry about the words of the elders, what Andrew or what Peter of what Philip or what Thomas or James or what John or Matthew or what any other of the disciples of the Lord said, also what Aristion and the Elder John, disciples of the Lord, say.[15]

14 Cf. Streeter, op. cit., pp. 442-447.
15 Lightfoot, op. cit., p. 516.

The apparently dual sense in which the word "elder" is used creates an ambiguity, and the repetition of the name "John", both times classed with the disciples of the Lord and with the "elders", aggravates the confusion. But surely the balance of probability falls on the side of the inference that he meant to designate a certain John, a personal disciple of Jesus, who was distinguished from the Apostle of the same name by the constant association of the title elder with his name—the Elder John, or just "The Elder", as distinct for the Apostle John.

But still another difficulty afflicts our hypothesis. Papias does not indicate definitely that the Elder John lived in Ephesus. Bacon has made out a very strong case for his residence in Jerusalem.[16] The basal predicate of our hypothesis, however, attaches a strong implication to the language of Papias which otherwise it would not possess. Assuming that the Apostle John was resident in Ephesus, then the distinguishing title for the other John would suggest that he lived in Ephesus also; otherwise, little need existed for so distinguishing him. Furthermore, it seems most probable that Papias was making his inquiries with a view to authenticating the tradition as it prevailed in Asia, where he himself resided and labored. On this supposition it would be most natural to consider Aristion and John the Elder as the last surviving authoritative sources of tradition in Papias' own time, and as Christian visitors or immigrants came from Ephesus to Hierapolis Papias availed himself of the opportunity thus afforded him to check up on items

16 Hibbert Journal, vol. xxix, pp. 812-826.

of tradition which were in doubt. This would explain the tenses of the Greek verbs used.

The complicated and speculative character of the hypothesis here offered we frankly recognize, and therefore would be far from insisting upon it as proven and final. It is offered as a suggestion which we believe to be in harmony with the traditional evidence of the second century and the phenomena of the Gospel itself. No theory of the authorship of the Fourth Gospel can ever be demonstrated with finality until evidence we do not now possess is brought to light. Conflicting inferences will continue to be drawn from the facts as we know them, and new implications and combinations of these facts will be exhibited, modifying the respective plausibility of different views, but nothing final can be proven from evidence as we know it now. It therefore behoves critics to be properly modest about their own findings and considerate toward the views and findings of others. There is no field of New Testament criticism in which it is more unbecoming to appear dogmatic about any favored theory.

BIBLIOGRAPHY

In the prepartation of this treatise the following works have been used.

SYNOPTIC PROBLEM

Burton, *Some Principles of Literary Criticism and Their Application To the Synoptic Problem* (Chicago, 1904)

Harnack, *Date of Acts and the Synoptic Gospels* (New York, 1911)
The Sayings of Jesus (New York, 1908)

Hawkins, *Horae Synopticae* (Oxford, 1909)

Petrie, *The Growth of the Gospels* (New York, 1911)

Sanday, *Studies In the Synoptic Problem* (Oxford, 1911)

Streeter, *The Four Gospels* (New York, 1925)

FORM CRITICISM

Bultmann, *Die Geschichte der synoptischen Tradition* (Goettingen, 1931)

Cadbury, *The Making of Luke-Acts* (New York, 1927)

Dibelius, *From Tradition To Gospel* (London, 1934)

Easton, *The Gospel Before the Gospels* (New York, 1928)

Filson, *Origins of the Gospels* (Cincinnati, 1938)

Grant, *Form Criticism* (Chicago, 1934)
    The Growth of the Gospels (Cincinnati, 1933)

Lightfoot, *History and Interpretation In the Gospels* (London, 1935)

Redlich: *Form Criticism: Its Value and Limitations* (New York, 1939)

Richardson, *The Gospels In the Making* (London, 1938)

Riddle, *The Gospels: Their Origin and Growth* (Chicago, 1939)

Scott, *The Validity of the Gospel Record* (New York, 1938)

Taylor, *The Formation of the Gospel Tradition* (London, 1935)

THE FOURTH GOSPEL

Bacon, *The Fourth Gospel In Research and Debate* (New York, 1910)
    The Gospel of the Hellenists (New York, 1933)

Bernard, "The Gospel of John" in *The International Critical Commentary* (Edinburgh, 1928)

Colwell, *The Greek of the Fourth Gospel* (Chicago, 1931)
    John Defends the Gospel (Chicago, 1936)

Dods, "The Gospel of John" in *The Expositor's Greek Testament* (Eerdmans, Grand Rapids, Michigan, reprint c. 1935)

Gardner-Smith, *St. John and the Synoptic Gospels* (Cambridge, 1938)

Howard, *The Fourth Gospel In Recent Criticism and Interpretation* (London, 1931)

Lewis, *Disarrangements of the Fourth Gospel* (Cambridge, 1910)

Macgregor, "The Gospel of John" in *The Moffatt New Testament Commentary* (London, 1928)

Redlich, *An Introduction To the Fourth Gospel* (London, 1939)

Sanday, *The Criticism of the Fourth Gospel* (New York, 1905)

Scott, *The Fourth Gospel: Its Purpose and Theology* (Edinburg, 1906)

Stanton, *The Gospels As Historical Documents*, vol. iii (Cambridge, 1920)

Streeter, *The Four Gospels*, part iii (New York, 1925)

Windisch, *Johannes und die Synoptiker: Untersuchungen zum Neuen Testament*, vol. xii (Leipsig, 1926)

RELATED WORKS

Bacon, *The Story of Jesus* (New York, 1927)

Dodd, *History and the Gospels* (New York, 1938)

Edersheim, *Life and Times of Jesus the Messiah* (New York, 1906)

Enslin, *Christian Beginnings* (New York, 1938)

Feine, *Einleitung in das Neue Testament* (Leipsig, 1922)

Foakes Jackson, 'The Acts of the Apostles" in *The Moffatt New Testament Commentary* (London, 1931)

Foakes Jackson and Lake, *The Beginnings of Christianity* (London, 1920-1933)

Goodspeed, *Introduction To the New Testament* (Chicago, 1937)

Gunkel, *Eucharisterion* (Gœttingen, 1923)

Harnack, *Bible Reading In the Early Church* (New York, 1912)

Hopwood, *The Religious Experience of the Primitive Church* (Edinburgh, 1936)

Kræling, *Anthropos and the Son of Man* (New York, 1927)

Lightfoot, *The Apostolic Fathers* (London, 1912)

Macdonald, *Christian Worship In the Primitive Church* (Edinburgh, 1934)

Moffatt, *Introduction To the Literature of the New Testament* (New York, 1911)

Oesterly and Box, *The Religion and Worship of the Synagogue* (London, 1911)

Peake, *Critical Introduction To the New Testament* (New York, 1910)

Roberts and Donaldson, *Ante-Nicene Fathers* (New York, 1899)

Schaff, *Nicene & Post-Nicene Fathers* (Buffalo, 1886)

Streeter, *The Primitive Church* (New York, 1929)

5